Great Medical Discoveries

Organ Transplants

by James Barter

LUCENT BOOKS
An imprint of Thomson Gale, a part of The Thomson Corporation

THOMSON
™
GALE

Detroit • New York • San Francisco • San Diego • New Haven, Conn. • Waterville, Maine • London • Munich

LIBRARY OF CONGRESS CATALOGING-IN-PUBLICATION DATA

Barter, James, 1946–
  Organ transplants / by James Barter.
    p. cm. — (Great medical discoveries)
  Includes bibliographical references and index.
  ISBN 1-59018-684-2 (hard cover : alk. paper)
  1. Transplantation of organs, tissues, etc.—Juvenile literature. I. Title. II. Series.
  RD120.76.B37 2005
  617.9'5—dc22
                                                          2005006306

Printed in the United States of America

CONTENTS

FOREWORD

Throughout history, people have struggled to understand and conquer the diseases and physical ailments that plague us. Once in a while, a discovery has changed the course of medicine and sometimes, the course of history itself. The stories of these discoveries have many elements in common—accidental findings, sudden insights, human dedication, and most of all, powerful results. Many illnesses that in the past were essentially a death warrant for their sufferers are today curable or even virtually extinct. And exciting new directions in medicine promise a future in which the building blocks of human life itself—the genes—may be manipulated and altered to restore health or to prevent disease from occurring in the first place.

It has been said that an insight is simply a rearrangement of already-known facts, and as often as not, these great medical discoveries have resulted partly from a reexamination of earlier efforts in light of new knowledge. Nineteenth-century monk Gregor Mendel experimented with pea plants for years, quietly unlocking the mysteries of genetics. However, the importance of his findings went unnoticed until three separate scientists, studying cell division with a newly improved invention called a microscope, rediscovered his work decades after his death. French doctor Jean-Antoine Villemin's experiments with rabbits proved that tuberculosis was contagious, but his conclusions were politely ignored by the medical community until another doctor, Robert Koch of Germany, discovered the exact culprit—the tubercle bacillus germ—years later.

Accident, too, has played a part in some medical discoveries. Because the tuberculosis germ does not stain with dye as easily as other bacteria, Koch was able to see it only after he had let a treated slide sit far longer than he intended. An unwanted speck of mold led Englishman Alexander Fleming to recognize the bacteria-killing qualities of the penicillium fungi, ushering in the era of antibiotic "miracle drugs."

That researchers sometimes benefited from fortuitous accidents does not mean that they were bumbling amateurs who relied solely on luck. They were dedicated scientists whose work created the conditions under which such lucky events could occur; many sacrificed years of their lives to observation and experimentation. Sometimes the price they paid was higher. Rene Launnec, who invented the stethoscope to help him study the effects of tuberculosis, himself succumbed to the disease.

And humanity has benefited from these scientists' efforts. The formerly terrifying disease of smallpox has been eliminated from the face of the earth—the only case of the complete conquest of a once deadly disease. Tuberculosis, perhaps the oldest disease known to humans and certainly one of its most prolific killers, has been essentially wiped out in some parts of the world. Genetically engineered insulin is a godsend to countless diabetics who are allergic to the animal insulin that has traditionally been used to help them.

Despite such triumphs there are few unequivocal success stories in the history of great medical discoveries. New strains of tuberculosis are proving to be resistant to the antibiotics originally developed to treat them, raising the specter of a resurgence of the disease that has killed 2 billion people over the course of human history. But medical research continues on numerous fronts and will no doubt lead to still undreamed-of advancements in the future.

Each volume in the Great Medical Discoveries series tells the story of one great medical breakthrough—the first gropings for understanding, the pieces that came together and how, and the immediate and longer-term results. Part science and part social history, the series explains some of the key findings that have shaped modern medicine and relieved untold human suffering. Numerous primary and secondary source quotations enhance the text and bring to life all the drama of scientific discovery. Sidebars highlight personalities and convey personal stories. The series also discusses the future of each medical discovery—a future in which vaccines may guard against AIDS, gene therapy may eliminate cancer, and other as-yet unimagined treatments may become commonplace.

INTRODUCTION

Assisting Bodies Beyond Repair

Organ transplantation was one of the major scientific accomplishments of the latter half of the twentieth century. Thanks to a generation of committed researchers and risk-taking surgeons, people suffering from irreparable organ failure have been saved by having someone else's healthy organ—a liver, kidney, lung, or heart—transplanted into their body.

For thousands of years before the twentieth century, physicians unschooled in science imagined saving lives by trading failed organs and limbs for new ones. First, however, doctors learned how to repair damaged organs—temporarily. With the advent of modern surgical procedures about one hundred years ago, doctors could repair a limited number of problems distressing the heart, lung, kidney, and liver. Unfortunately, for most patients who underwent surgical procedures to heal their organs, their lives were only briefly extended. In many cases, vital organs recuperated for a year or two only to fail again.

It was not until the beginning of the twentieth century that physicians considered an entirely new idea for dealing with seriously diseased organs. Researchers looked for ways of removing unhealthy organs and replacing them with healthy ones. Dozens of medical research teams pondered and solved myriad problems involved in this procedure. Their work led to the first successful kidney transplant in 1954, followed thirteen years later by the first heart transplant. Since those two revolutionary surgeries, doctors have transplanted tens of thousands of kidneys, hearts, lungs, livers, colons, pancreases, and other organs. In 2004 alone, organ transplants extended the lives of twenty-five thousand Americans.

By any measure, organ transplants are a remarkable achievement. Yet they remain an imperfect solution. The demand for healthy organs is high, the supply limited, and ensuring the body's acceptance of donated organs still presents problems for patients and their

A team of surgeons prepares a donor heart to be transplanted into the body of a recipient.

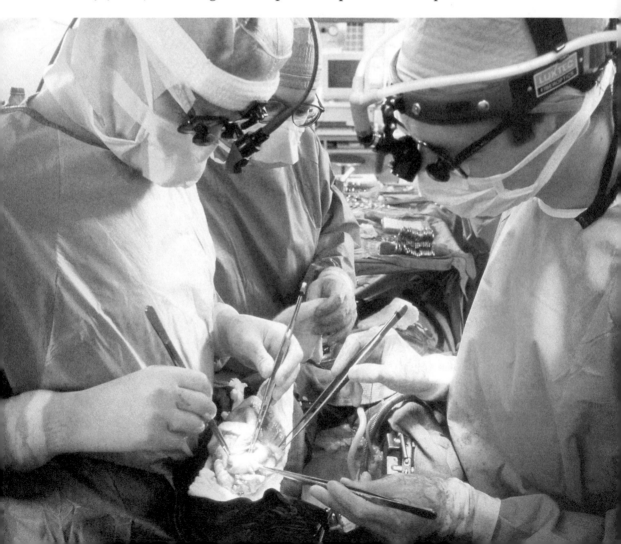

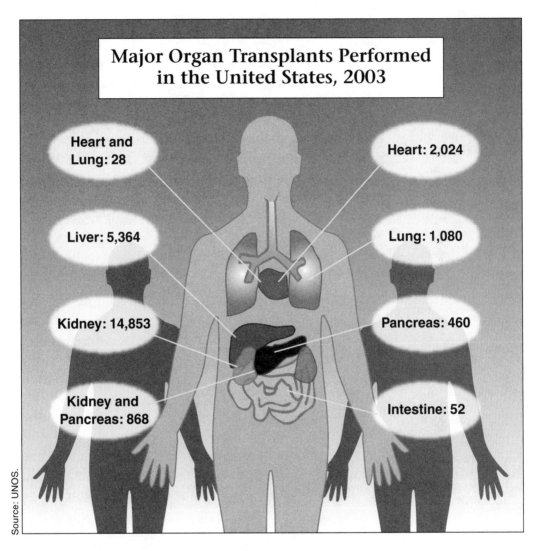

Major Organ Transplants Performed in the United States, 2003

Heart and Lung: 28

Heart: 2,024

Liver: 5,364

Lung: 1,080

Kidney: 14,853

Pancreas: 460

Kidney and Pancreas: 868

Intestine: 52

Source: UNOS.

doctors. For these and other reasons, philosophy professor and medical writer Ronald Munson calls transplantation

a crude, stop-gap measure to keep people from dying. *Really* successful transplantation would solve the problem it's intended to solve without generating others. It would give [patients] a new heart without turning them into patients with chronic illnesses. It would restore [them] to health and be so free of negative fallout it would resemble magic. [1]

Scientists are confident they can deliver the magic within the next two decades. The magic being proposed and developed in laboratories around the world is revolutionary because it no longer involves donations of human organs, the weak link in the present system. Modern researchers are pinning their hopes on a variety of technologies to develop organs that are mechanical, harvested from animal organ farms, cloned, or produced in laboratories from a patient's own body cells. Munson supports this array of leading-edge technologies, concluding, "If we don't do this, the magic will never happen."[2]

CHAPTER 1

The First Attempts at Transplants

B efore physicians could feel confident about performing organ transplants on their human patients, they first needed to experiment on animals. They understood that animal organs were very different and less complex than those of humans, yet animal experiments would reveal much needed information. This information came first from animal-to-animal transplants and then from animal-to-human transplants.

Animal-to-Animal Transplants

Toward the end of the nineteenth century, a group of European doctors speculated in medical journals about the possibilities of transplanting organs from one animal to another. They were aware of earlier transplantations of simple tissues, such as skin and muscle, but understood that the transplantation of an entire vital organ would be far more complex. They further understood that they could learn many lessons from organ transplants in animals without placing human lives at risk.

The first successful operation transplanting a whole organ from one animal to another was done by the Austrian physician Emerich Ullman. In March 1902, he reported the results of this operation, which involved the transfer of a kidney from one dog to another. This procedure was an allograft, meaning a transplant from one animal to another, genetically unrelated animal.

During the surgery, Ullman removed a kidney from one dog and transplanted it into the neck of another. Why Ullman chose the neck is not explained in his journal but it probably allowed him to keep the kidney alive for a period of time. Within the neck are major arteries that pump blood through the body. Ullman's journal states that the kidney continued to function normally during the experimental procedure. His decision to join the kidney to the neck may have had something to do with this. He also connected a tube to the kidney for drainage. The tube protruded through the animal's skin; urine generated by the kidney as it filtered impurities from the blood drained out the tube.

Emboldened by his success with the dog-to-dog kidney transplant, Ullman then experimented with kidney transplants from dogs to goats. He reported similar successes with these transplants. In the several dozen kidney transplants that Ullman performed, he reported that the transplanted kidneys functioned properly, although most of the animals did not live long.

While Ullman and others were attempting to improve kidney transplants, the French physician Alexis Carrel and his colleagues tackled the much more complicated experiment of transplanting a heart between two dogs. In 1905, Carrel removed the heart of a small dog and transplanted it into a larger one. He attached the heart by suturing together the cut ends of the veins and arteries. The dog survived the operation, but blood clots in the cavities of the transplanted heart killed the dog about two hours later.

A year later Carrel reported that he had transplanted the heart and lungs of a week-old cat into the neck of an adult cat. As Ullman had done before him, Carrel attached the heart using the major arteries of the neck. He stated, "We attempted also to make the transplantation of the lungs together with the heart. Both lungs, the heart, the aorta, and vena cava [the two largest veins in the body] of a cat one week old were extirpated [removed] and put into the neck of a large adult cat."[3] Details for such complex surgery are lacking but he reported that blood circulation was immediately reestablished, and the lungs became red with oxygenated blood after a few minutes. Despite these initial signs of success, the cat died a short time later.

In 1905 French physician Alexis Carrel transplanted the heart of a small dog into a larger one. Although the procedure was a success, the large dog died from complications.

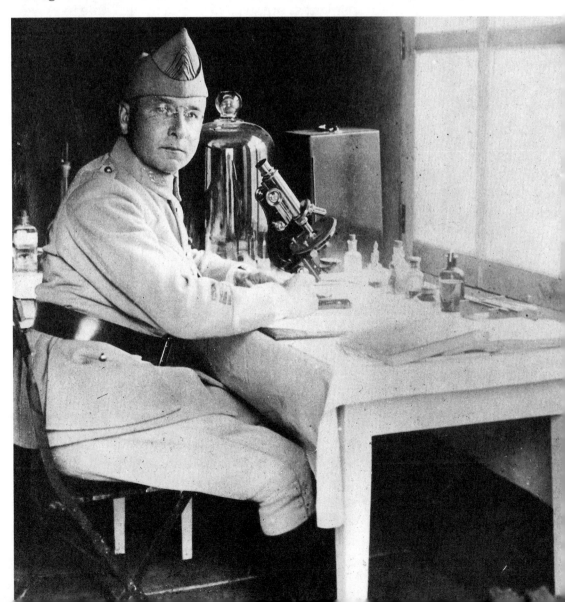

Carrel also performed a third transplant. This time he removed one kidney from a dog and transplanted it to a different location in the same dog, a procedure called an autograft. This dog survived for several months.

Autopsies on the animals helped Ullman and Carrel identify three problems. The first was that neither physician had successfully joined the animals' blood vessels with the transplanted organs. Internal bleeding was the result. The second problem was that the transplanted organs had begun to die while they were being transferred from the donor to the recipient animal. Tissue discoloration confirmed the need for a means of preserving organs while they were disconnected from the body's nourishing blood supply.

The third problem presented the physicians with a mystery. The difficulty of joining the organs to the body's blood vessels and preserving the organs until the operation was completed did not fully explain why the organs failed within a few days or months of transplantation. In most cases, once the kidneys were implanted, the tissue gained its normal color and the

Alexis Carrel

Alexis Carrel was born in 1873 in a suburb of Lyon, France. As a boy, Alexis learned from his seamstress mother how to sew fine silk and linen materials. These skills would later play a role in his success as an inventive surgeon.

According to historians, Carrel's interest in surgical techniques was piqued in 1894 when the president of France bled to death after being wounded in an assassination attempt in Lyon. Carrel understood that if doctors had known how to suture the president's sliced arteries, his life could have been saved. Because of this violent event, Carrel committed himself to finding a way to sew severed blood vessels back together.

In 1906 Carrel moved to New York to work at the prestigious Rockefeller Institute for Medical Research. There he perfected artery suturing and organ perfusion, both necessary for organ transplantation. In addition, Carrel continued to experiment with a variety of human and animal organ transplantations in hopes of solving the problem of organ rejection. In 1941, when France was occupied by the German army during World War II, Carrel felt compelled to return to Paris to lend medical aid to the French. In 1944, he died in Paris from a heart attack.

kidneys generated urine—two unmistakable signs of normal kidney function. Yet the kidneys had failed. Carrel was determined to find out why. First, however, he tackled the two more easily corrected problems.

Alexis Carrel demonstrates to students at the Rockefeller Institute how to suture wounds using fine threads of silk.

Lessons Learned from the Early Experiments

In 1906, Carrel set to work on the problem of how to attach the veins and arteries of transplanted organs to those of the recipient's body. Carrel was the son of a seamstress and as a boy had learned many techniques for sewing delicate silk cloth using the fewest and smallest stitches possible. He experimented with several techniques before developing the method of joining blood vessels end to end, a procedure called anastomosis. Using fine threads made of silk and dipped in petroleum jelly to sterilize them, he sutured the blood vessels end to end using just three stitches. His sutures eventually held well enough for the blood

Carrel's Celebrated Suture

Carrel's success with suturing blood vessels together was the result of his discovery of a technique called triangulation suturing. The essence of the suture was to sew the ends of vessels together along straight lines instead of sewing around in a circle. The technique was described at the 1912 Nobel Prize ceremony. According to the Nobel Prize Web site, "The French doctor, when he made a suture, enlarged the opening using three retaining stitches located at equidistant points which converted the round opening into a triangular one, following which he stitched the walls together again edge to edge with fine silk threaded on to ordinary needles, which were very fine and round."

to circulate without leaking while the two conjoined vessels healed together to create a strong, permanent seam in the vessel.

Many surgeons consider Carrel's technique for connecting blood vessels one of the great surgical achievements of the twentieth century. In 1912, the discovery of this successful procedure earned Carrel the Nobel Prize in Physiology or Medicine.

Following his discovery of anastomosis, Carrel set to work on the second transplant problem both he and Ullman had encountered—preserving organs *ex corporeal* (Latin for "outside the body"). Physicians had known for a long time that organs could not live for more than five or ten minutes apart from the body. Carrel correctly observed that until organs could be preserved outside of a body for substantially longer periods, human organ transplants would never become a reality.

Some solution would need to be found for keeping organ tissue alive for an hour or more while the organ transfer took place. Initial experiments by Carrel revealed that tissue survived longer when stored at low temperatures. Experimenting with animal organs, Carrel found that the colder the temperature, the longer the organs could be preserved without damage. But when he froze organs, he could not revitalize them.

Through his experiments, Carrel found that the optimal temperature for preserving *ex corporeal* organs was just two degrees above freezing. At that temperature, some vital organs could survive for up to thirty minutes because their metabolism slows down and the need for oxygen and nutrients lessens.

Carrel also recognized that, in addition to lowering organ temperatures, artificially replicating the internal environment of circulating blood would be necessary outside the body. Carrel struck up a friendship with the famed American aviator Charles Lindbergh and the two collaborated on a simple mechanical pump to circulate a nutrient-rich, blood-based liquid through organs, a procedure called perfusion. The use of the

Aviator Charles Lindbergh (left) and Alexis Carrel (right) collaborated to develop a mechanical blood pump that prolonged the life of organs outside the body.

perfusion pump, combined with lowering the organ temperature, extended *ex corporeal* tissue life of many animal organs for more than an hour. A reporter who saw the perfusion pump described it:

> Looking like a twist of vitrified [glass] bowel oozing out of a clear glass bottle, the Lindbergh perfusion pump consists of three chambers one above the other. The organ to be studied lies on the slanting glass floor of the topmost [chamber]. Nutritious fluid from the lowest or reservoir chamber is driven up a glass tube connected with the organ's artery, to and through the organ by pulsating gas pressure. [4]

Carrel believed that he may have improved the likelihood for successful organ transplants. To test his hypothesis, he carried out heart transplants between animals. Each time, the procedure seemed a success, with a vital, beating, transplanted heart and no internal blood loss. Yet each time, the animal died within two or three days. Clearly, a key piece of information was missing.

In Carrel's 1912 Nobel Prize speech, he said that the technical problems of transplantation were essentially solved, but that some mysterious reaction within patients was still causing organ failures. Until some method was developed to prevent what appeared to be an adverse reaction of the recipient's system against the foreign tissue, organ transplants would not be possible.

> Before this [a successful kidney transplant] is accomplished it will be necessary to discover a means of recognizing the individuals, if such exist, between whom organs can be interchanged . . . Thus, while the problem of the transplantation of organs has been solved from a surgical point of view, we see that this by no means suffices to render such operations of definite surgical practicability, and it will only be through a more fundamental study of the biological relationships existing between living tissues that the problems involved will come to be solved and thereby render possible the benefits to humanity which we hope to see accomplished in the future. [5]

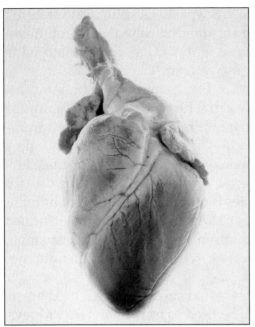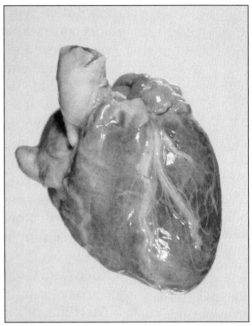

The First Animal-to-Human Transplants

While Ullman and Carrel were doing their ground-breaking work, other physicians began experiments with animal-to-human organ transplants. This procedure is known as xenotransplantation. Sheep and pigs were considered good candidates because their organs are similar in size and physiology to human organs, and the supply is plentiful. Physicians believed that animals with organs similar to those of humans might keep desperately ill patients alive until the science of transplanting organs from human donors could be perfected.

The first doctor to perform a xenotransplantation was Mathieu Jaboulay, a professor of surgery in Lyon, France. In 1906, he transplanted the kidney of a sheep into one patient and the kidney of a pig into another. Both patients were dying of kidney failure. After the surgery, each patient survived for one day before dying for reasons not understood at the time. In 1909, a French team of surgeons transplanted the kidney of a rabbit into a child suffering from kidney failure. Although the immediate results were excellent, the

Because a pig heart (left) is similar to the human heart (right), researchers concluded that pigs would make strong candidates for animal-to-human transplants.

child died within two weeks. Despite these failures, surgeons realized for the first time that organ transplants could succeed and one day might succeed in sustaining life for many years.

That same year, Dr. Ernst Unger of Germany came up with a new idea that he believed might stem the streak of xenotransplant failures. He proposed transplanting an ape kidney into a young girl with failing kidneys. Unger theorized that the use of a primate kidney might increase the chances for success because the anatomy of primates is more similar to that of humans than the anatomies of lower mammals. He performed the operation but within a few days the transplanted kidney became swollen, ceased urine production, ruptured, and the girl died.

Convinced that he could succeed, Unger tried again. This time, though, he tried to transplant two kidneys. Since people normally have two kidneys, he thought

A team of surgeons transplants the liver of a baboon into a human in 1992. German physician Ernst Unger first theorized in 1909 that ape-to-human transplants might be viable.

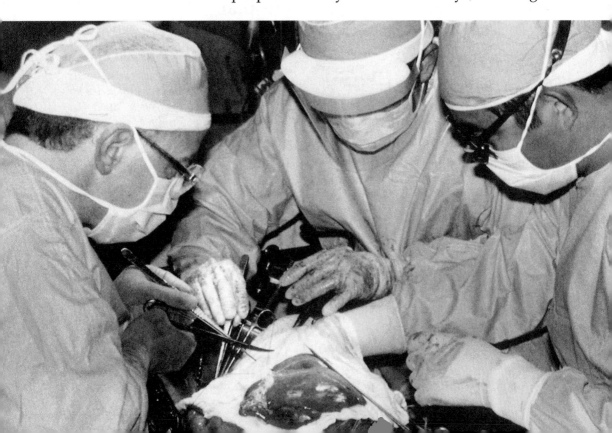

this might increase the chance of survival. In 1910 he transplanted two kidneys from a monkey into a twenty-year-old ill patient. Contrary to Unger's theory, these kidneys never properly functioned and the patient died thirty-two hours later.

The dismal results of xenotransplants continued. Unger and others tried other animal kidneys using various surgical procedures in hopes of finding a combination that might work. No successful combination was found. In the opinion of Dr. Luis H. Toledo-Pereyra, who studied the history of xenotransplants and wrote several years later, "Failure after failure greatly discouraged the few surgeons still interested in the transplantation of animal organs into humans suffering from irreversible kidney disease."[6]

Some people outside the medical profession accepted the failures of xenotransplantation with a sense of satisfaction. Although physicians held the view that their experiments would one day save lives, others believed that implanting animal organs inside people was not only bizarre, but morally reprehensible.

Moral Outrage

Xenotransplantation surgeons eager to push their nascent technology forward collided with people who expressed outrage at the idea of transplanting animal organs into humans. According to Bernard E. Rollin, professor of biomedical sciences at Cambridge University in England, newspapers following the first xenotransplants carried stories about people who believed that physicians were attempting to create Frankenstein monsters that would be neither human nor animal. In his book *The Frankenstein Syndrome: Ethical and Social Issues in the Genetic Engineering of Animals,* Rollin notes, "The first pig organs transplanted into humans raised a hue and cry [alarm] across the land. Societies to curb the use of animal organs sprang up, fearing humans would become only partial humans."[7]

Most upset were members of the clergy. Citing Biblical references that differentiate humans from animals and signify that humans were intended to be dominant over animals, religious leaders argued that humans were not meant to live with the assistance of animal organs. To do so, they insisted, would violate the word of God and debase humans, making them something less than what God had intended. Religious leaders admired the work of physicians curing people of diseases and repairing diseased organs, but the implantation of animal organs was seen as sacrilege.

People outside the clergy also expressed discomfort with the idea of saving human lives with animal organs. At a fundamental level, xenotransplants seemed to transgress boundaries that define humans as a unique species, therefore challenging and threatening people's identity and sense of being a human. Many openly admitted to a queasy feeling at the thought of animal organs inside their bodies. Some early twentieth-century anthropologists joined the ethical debate, suggesting that people receiving animal organs might be very different following their surgery. These anthropologists argued that people's understandings of their world were the result of their unique organs and that people receiving animal organs might acquire a very different understanding of the world. The notion of acquiring animal characteristics was a source of terror and revulsion that prompted many to express a preference for death over living with an animal organ.

Some medical ethicists, physicians who debate the ethical principles of medical procedures and laws, worried about possible health risks. Animals were known to carry diseases unique to their species, raising the concern that animal organs introduced into humans might spread those diseases to humans. Indeed, ethicists feared that a new plague might erupt, similar to ones in the past that wiped out millions of people. Only this time, a plague might be transmitted by people whose bodies contained animal organs, not by animals.

According to one journalist investigating this idea at the time, "No, this is not an unrealistic possibility. There are large numbers of diseases which affect other animals and not humans, but that may change if we start putting their organs in our bodies."[8]

As the debate raged, an important discovery took place in one of the laboratories of the Department of Pathological Anatomy at the University of Vienna in Austria. It appeared that a Viennese physician had made the discovery that might explain Carrel's reference to adverse reactions in his Nobel Prize speech. Many doctors thought this discovery might finally unlock the door to the first successful transplant.

Discovery of Blood Types

The Viennese physician, Karl Landsteiner, was performing pioneering work on blood transfusions in 1910. For reasons unknown to him, some recipients of blood experienced severe adverse reactions, culminating in death, while others experienced a new vitality. Landsteiner had read about the problems associated with early organ transplants and became interested in knowing whether the blood in animals and humans was the same. If not, he theorized, different types of blood might partially explain why early organ transplants had failed, apart from Carrel's one exception of a transplant within the same animal.

Through his experiments, Landsteiner discovered that there are differences in the make up of human and animal blood. He then turned his attention to human blood, leading this time to the discovery that two people could have different blood chemistry. To determine the effects on a person experiencing the mixing of two different types of blood, Landsteiner mixed blood from two individuals in a glass beaker and studied the results under a microscope. Unlike blood cells taken from the same person, which remain detached from other cells, the mixed blood cells clumped together in a process known as agglutination. Landsteiner further observed that clumped cells cracked and emitted toxins in the blood that could have fatal consequences.

Following six years of laboratory tests, Landsteiner discovered that all human blood could be classified into four basic types that he labeled A, B, AB, and O. Furthermore, Landsteiner realized that each of these four types has what he called chemical factors that are either negative or positive. Safe transfusions of blood required that the donor and recipient have both a compatible blood type and a compatible chemical factor, meaning that some combinations were safe yet most were not. Compatibility was later shown to be a requirement not only for blood transfusions but for organ transplantation as well.

Many surgeons believed that Landsteiner had solved the mystery that had earlier stumped Carrel. Optimism surged among surgeons bent on attempting the first human-to-human organ transplants.

The First Human-to-Human Transplants

The first few attempts at kidney transplants between humans were disasters. Physicians in the early 1930s mistakenly believed that they understood all the complexities of organ transplants and set out to prove that the time had arrived for this new branch of medicine.

The first to attempt an organ transplant between humans was a Ukrainian surgeon, Yu Yu Voronoy, in 1933. Six coal miners came to his clinic dying from chloride and mercury poisoning that destroyed most of their kidney tissue. Just by chance, Voronoy also had a patient who had been involved in an automobile accident and was dying. But the patient's kidneys were healthy. In a snap decision, Voronoy decided to try transplanting the kidneys of his dying patient into one of the miners who seemed to have a compatible blood type. Voronoy operated as soon as the donor patient died. Within three days the recipient patient also died. Voronoy attempted human kidney transplants five more times over the next few years—all with the same results. None of the

Karl Landsteiner

Karl Landsteiner began his study of blood as a medical student at the University of Vienna in Austria. His studies of blood chemistry took him to Munich, Germany, where he worked in several medical laboratories.

He was known as a meticulous researcher. This quality, more than any other, led to his greatest finding, the discovery of multiple human blood types. Landsteiner was the first to study the reactions of patients who had received blood transfusions. He pointed out that unless the blood types were compatible, shock, jaundice, and death would follow. His research received little attention until he classified the blood of human beings into the now well-known A, B, AB, and O groups. He received the Nobel Prize for this work. Without this discovery, organ transplantation could not have advanced as it did.

Austrian physician Karl Landsteiner discovered that there are four basic human blood types, each incompatible with the other.

transplanted healthy kidneys functioned. He was baffled by the failures because he had carefully performed the mechanics of the operations and believed he had matched the blood types properly.

In 1952, a French physician, Jean Hamburger, made another attempt at a human kidney transplant. While working in a Boston hospital, he transplanted a kidney taken from a traffic accident victim into her son, who had survived the accident but suffered severe kidney damage. At the end of the second week, the surgical team was elated with their success, but by the beginning of the fourth week failure again struck.

Although Hamburger experienced greater success than Voronoy, it was clear to surgeons that some key piece of information about organ transplantation was

In 1952 French physician Jean Hamburger performed a successful human-to-human kidney transplant. A few weeks later, however, the patient died from organ failure.

still missing. It seemed apparent that the surgical techniques for transplantation of kidneys could be mastered, but the problem of preventing organ failure appeared insurmountable. As more kidney transplants failed, French physiologist Dr. René Küss summarized the state of affairs in the early 1950s by observing, "The results from medical teams in France as well as the United States led us to believe that transplant surgery was impossible."[9]

Unknown to doctors at the time, the critical piece of information that would explain all the kidney failures in animals and humans had been discovered but had not yet been published. That finding, carried out by Peter Medawar, a Lebanese physician working in England in the mid-1940s, held the missing key to the first successful kidney transplant.

CHAPTER 2

The Problem Within

The research performed by Dr. Medawar revealed that the last remaining obstacle to successful organ transplantations resides within people's bodies. That obstacle is the immune system which functions as the body's security force. It protects the body by detecting and destroying foreign tissues and microorganisms that enter the body. From the standpoint of the immune system, transplanted organs are alien invaders that have to be destroyed.

Discovering the Mysterious Immune System

The discovery of the immune system took place during World War II. At the time the British government was concerned about the large number of soldiers and civilians dying from severe burns. Medawar was asked to aid in the war effort by studying ways that skin grafts, or transplants, could help heal burned skin.

Medawar had read Carrel's papers and was especially interested in his one success with an autograft kidney transplant. Medawar had performed enough skin transplants to know that autografted skin (skin from the patient's own body) successfully heals burns while allografted skin (skin from someone else) quickly discolors, shrivels, and dies. While puzzling over this phenomenon, Medawar made two crucial discoveries.

In the course of doing allografts on animal embryos just a few weeks old, Medawar discovered that their young systems did not react adversely to foreign tissues. Yet when he conducted the same allograft transplants on older animals, the transplant tissues died after a few weeks. Based on these differing observations, Medawar concluded that something was occurring in animals later in development that caused their bodies to kill the grafted skin tissues.

Through his pioneering work with skin grafts, Dr. Peter Medawar discovered the existence of the human body's immune system.

Medawar then conducted a second set of allograft transplants exclusively on mature animals in the hopes of uncovering the baffling reason tissues died. After many experiments, he found that the second time an animal received an allograft, the transplanted tissue survived for just a few days rather than weeks, as was the case following the first transplant. For some reason, the allograft tissues died more quickly after the animal's second exposure. It was as if their bodies had learned some lesson from the first encounter. But how could that be possible?

After pondering his results, Medawar concluded that animals must possess some sort of identification mechanism that differentiates their own tissues from foreign tissues. Furthermore, the body's ability to make the differentiation matures after the embryonic stage. Medawar further deduced that once this identification mechanism detected alien tissue, it then set in motion a series of actions aimed at destroying the foreign invader. Medawar realized that this identification mechanism was capable of some sort of memory, which explained why it responded much more quickly following a second encounter.

Medawar called the complex system capable of identifying and attacking alien tissue "a mechanism of active immunization."[10] Later physicians simply called it the immune system.

The Immune System

Medawar's research to understand the immune system revealed that it consists of what physicians call the body's "second fluid system," the first being the blood. Both the blood and the immune system circulate chemical and biological agents throughout the body. The immune system does this work by way of the lymph system.

The lymph system consists primarily of lymph, lymph vessels, lymph nodes, and the spleen. Lymph is a clear, mucous-like fluid carrying white blood cells

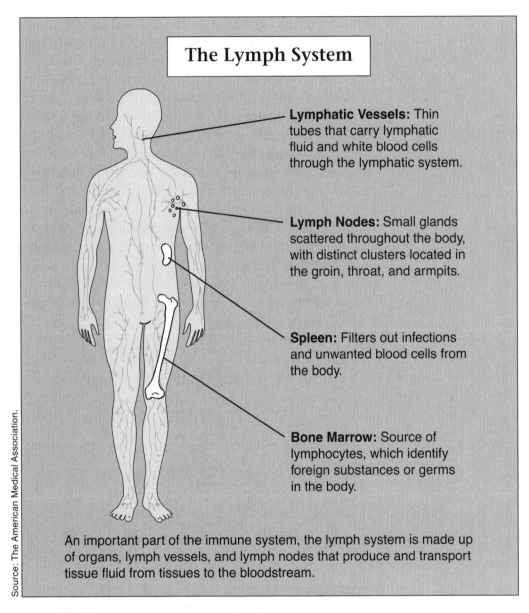

The Lymph System

Lymphatic Vessels: Thin tubes that carry lymphatic fluid and white blood cells through the lymphatic system.

Lymph Nodes: Small glands scattered throughout the body, with distinct clusters located in the groin, throat, and armpits.

Spleen: Filters out infections and unwanted blood cells from the body.

Bone Marrow: Source of lymphocytes, which identify foreign substances or germs in the body.

An important part of the immune system, the lymph system is made up of organs, lymph vessels, and lymph nodes that produce and transport tissue fluid from tissues to the bloodstream.

Source: The American Medical Association.

called lymphocytes. The lymphocytes are produced in bone marrow, the nutrient-rich, spongy tissue located in the center of bones. They are stored in the lymph nodes, which are small bean-shaped glands usually less than 0.5 inch (1 cm) in diameter. The lymph nodes are scattered throughout the body; most nodes are solitary but some are found in large clusters. Distinct concentrations of clusters are located in the groin, throat, and armpits. Since there is no pump such as the heart to circulate lymph, the system depends upon physical activity to move the clear fluid along a network of vessels. Unlike blood, lymph does not recirculate. It is eventually absorbed by the blood system and filtered from the body by the spleen.

Medawar and his colleagues noticed a connection between infections, indicating an invasion of foreign tissue, and swollen lymph glands. Patients with high fever—a sign that they had infection—also had swollen lymph glands. Medawar concluded that the swelling was a sign that the glands were producing more lymphocytes than normal. The swelling seemed to be a means for the body to squeeze high concentrations of lymphocytes into the lymph vessels that carried them to the site of the infection.

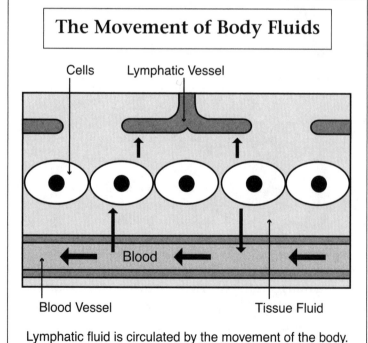

The Movement of Body Fluids

Cells   Lymphatic Vessel

Blood Vessel   Tissue Fluid

Lymphatic fluid is circulated by the movement of the body. One-way valves in the lymphatic vessels keep the fluids flowing in the right direction.

Source: The American Medical Association.

Differentiating Friendly from Foreign Tissue

Once Medawar correctly identified the connection between an infection and the increased activity of the lymph system, his next step was to explain how this system operates.

Medawar and his colleagues knew they were close to a major breakthrough. If they could explain the functioning of the immune system, they might be able to conduct successful organ transplants. To accomplish this, they had to look deep within the cells.

Medawar and his team of immunologists used microscopes and chemical analyses to identify a specific chemical pattern of molecules coating the surface of every human cell. These molecules, called major histocompatibility antigens (MHAs), have a particular structure unique to each individual. Once this piece of information was revealed, Medawar understood how the body's immune system recognizes foreign tissue.

Medawar discovered that the immune system functioned much like a well-coordinated security force. The lymphocytes intercept cells while they flow and chemically interrogate them to find out if they have MHAs different from their own. This constant vigilance is performed by five types of white blood cells, each playing a different role in identifying, destroying, and eliminating alien cells. Up to one trillion lymphocytes normally course through a person's body in search of microorganisms, tissue or other intruders that do not belong. When invaders are discovered, the lymph glands triple the number of lymphocytes. Their ultimate objective is to attack and kill alien cells without damaging their own tissue, a reaction physicians call rejection.

Organ Rejection

The process of organ rejection involves all the major lymphocytes, but three in particular play a critical role: B cells, T cells, and macrophages. The B cells, so named because they are produced and matured in the bone marrow, are the sentinel cells. They are the first to encounter and identify alien MHAs. When B cells encounter foreign cells, they engulf and mark them for destruction by attaching antibodies, chemical substances that begin the process of weakening the invaders. B cells live for a very long time and for this reason they are capable of "remembering" first encounters with foreign MHAs. This is what triggers a more rapid response in subsequent encounters.

The T cells, named for the thymus gland, located in the chest, are the warrior cells. Their main function is to seek out unfamiliar tissues marked by the B cells with antibodies. Once T cells encounter cells tagged with antibodies, they kill them by splitting them open, a process called lysing. The elapsed time from initial recognition to the lysing of the cell wall is about thirty minutes. T cells have the secondary responsibility of shutting down an immune response once they are unable to locate any more tagged intruders.

Macrophages, which take their name from Greek words meaning "large eaters," are scavengers. They are exceptionally large cells chemically programmed to locate and engulf dead and dying cells lysed by T cells. Once they engulf cells, macrophages release packets of enzymes that devour dead and dying invading cells along with the body's naturally dying cells.

Medawar correctly concluded that the rejection problem presented a formidable barrier to successful organ transplantation. When an organ was implanted, the highly sophisticated immune system would somehow need to be neutralized, or deceived into "thinking" that the foreign organ was actually its own. If that could not be accomplished, organ transplants would never succeed.

Medawar's work was revolutionary yet still untested. To prove his theory about the functioning of the immune system, one final test remained. Many surgeons had shown that allografts of kidneys failed, but no one had yet demonstrated that a kidney autograft could succeed. Autograft skin transplants had been successful, but skin is a very simple tissue compared to the complexities of a kidney. Medawar wondered how he could test the success of an autograft kidney transplant. Finding a subject for this procedure seemed unlikely because it would require the transplant of a kidney from its normal position in the body to another location in the same body. Such an operation made no sense until 1954, when a highly unlikely situation presented itself as the perfect test.

An Opportunity Arises

In 1954, Medawar's research on failed kidney transplants caught the attention of Dr. Joseph E. Murray. Murray had a patient suffering from failing kidneys. The patient, twenty-four-year-old Richard Herrick, had been forced to retire from his work with the U.S. Coast Guard in Boston because of chronic nephritis, an inflammation of the kidneys that threatened his life.

What made Herrick unusual was that he had an identical twin brother with two healthy kidneys. Murray had studied Medawar's research on the cause of organ rejection and understood that it occurred under all circumstances when the donor and recipient had different MHAs. Murray knew that because the two brothers had developed from the same egg within their mother, both had identical genetic structures. Murray concluded that because the twin brothers had the same genetic structure, they might also have identical MHAs. He had stumbled upon the perfect test for Medawar's research.

Murray approached Herrick's twin brother, Ronald, about donating one of his two healthy kidneys. Murray explained that Ronald could expect to live a normal life with just one healthy kidney. (People have two kidneys from birth but can live with only one.) Since their genetic makeup was believed to be identical, this

Ronald Herrick shows a nurse a picture of his twin brother Richard, to whom he donated a kidney in 1954.

transplant would be an autograft with a slight twist. Technically it was called the first isograft transplant, the transplantation of identical tissue from one person to another. To test his theory that identical twins would have the same MHAs, Murray performed a series of procedures. He later recalled in his autobiography, *Surgery of the Soul,* "To test the true genetic identity of these twin brothers, we performed 17 formal genetic tests, only one of which—the reciprocal skin grafts— provided indisputable evidence. After four weeks a skin graft from Ronald to Richard showed no sign of rejection."[11]

Ethical Concerns

Right up to the time of the kidney transplant, Murray and his team heard objections from some within the medical profession. The ethical questions did not address Richard because without the transplant he would have died. They focused instead on the removal of Ronald's healthy kidney.

A few surgeons objected to the operation on the grounds that the removal of the healthy kidney might jeopardize Ronald's life. If he contracted a kidney disease in the future, he might die. Without his second kidney, they argued, Ronald was running a risk of death. These physicians cited one of the most well–known ethical restrictions placed on doctors—to "do no harm." In the opinion of some, Murray would be violating that oath.

Questions about the psychological state of the patients were raised along with surgical ones. Henry M. Fox, chief of psychiatry at Peter Bent Brigham Hospital and one of the doctors monitoring the case, opposed the operation. He expressed concerns about subjecting Ronald to the stress of making such a decision:

> The important question would seem to be whether we as physicians have the right to put the healthy twin under the pressure of being asked whether he is willing to make this sacrifice. I do not feel that we have this right in view of the potential danger to the healthy twin as well as the uncertainty of the outcome for this patient. [12]

The ethical question was ultimately resolved by the family. Murray and other surgeons discussed the pros and cons of the operation with family members. In the end, Richard and Ronald decided to go forward with the surgery and other family members concurred. Just days before the scheduled operation, however, Richard sent a note to his brother to pack his bags and flee from the hospital. Ronald responded with his own note saying, "I am here and I am going to stay." [13]

The First Successful Kidney Transplant

The operation, scheduled for December 23, 1954, had become a media event. As Dr. Murray drove to Peter Bent Brigham Hospital that day, he listened to news about the operation on the radio. The general public seemed to understand that the transplant between the brothers might be the first successful transplant. Many hoped that success would lead to organ transplants for others in need.

By the time Murray arrived, two operating teams were assembled in adjoining surgery rooms, one for each brother. The operation began at 8:15 A.M. and by 9:45 Murray had exposed Richard's diseased kidneys and was ready to remove them. At that moment, Murray signaled to the other surgical team that it was time to remove the left kidney from Ronald. Ronald's surgeon carried the healthy organ, immersed in a bath of near freezing water and nutrients, from one operating arena to the other. At 10:10 Murray inserted the kidney in Richard and began the lengthy process of connecting all the major blood vessels. To avoid spilling blood during the procedure, Murray clamped the vessels. The kidney was therefore without blood and, as he worked, it began to turn a grayish color, indicating distress. At 11:15, Murray completed all vessel attachments and released the clamps. In his autobiography, Murray recalled that moment:

When Kidneys Fail

Kidneys filter 400 gallons (1,520 liters) of blood each day to remove excess fluid, minerals, medications, and other wastes from the blood. They also produce hormones that strengthen bones and promote healthy blood. When kidneys fail, harmful wastes build up in the body, causing blood pressure to rise and insufficient red blood cells to form. The most common solution for kidney failure is to visit a hospital two to three times a week to have blood filtered by a dialysis machine.

Each year, approximately 217,000 Americans undergo kidney dialysis. During the three-hour procedure, one tube draws contaminated blood to the dialysis machine and a second tube returns clean blood to the patient.

Dialysis is only a temporary solution. A patient's energy levels following dialysis are high but within twelve hours, as the blood again absorbs waste products, the patient begins to tire. As more waste builds up during the next twelve hours, the patient struggles to maintain enough energy to work and carry on normal activities. By the time of the next dialysis session, most patients are not able to drive themselves to the hospital.

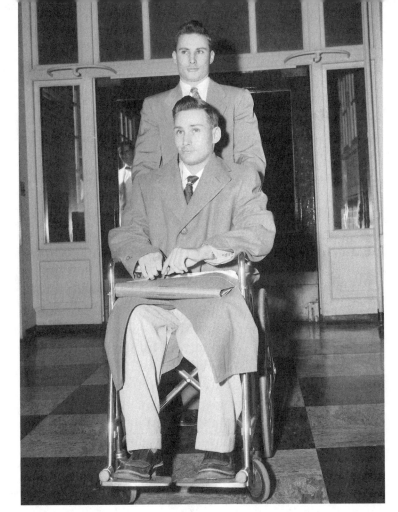

Ronald Herrick wheels his brother out of the hospital after the successful kidney transplant.

There was a collective hush in the operating room as we gently removed the clamps from the vessels newly attached to the donor kidney. As blood flow was restored, Richard's new kidney began to become engorged and turn pink. The donor kidney had been without blood flow for a total of 1 hour and 22 minutes. There were grins all around. We removed the remaining clamp from the common iliac artery approximately 10 minutes later and immediately noted pulsation.[14]

Within minutes, the kidney produced healthy urine. But the real test, whether rejection would occur, could not be confirmed for at least two weeks. When two weeks passed, doctors announced the successful transplantation to the world. After four weeks of close observation, both brothers were released from the hospital, free to resume their lives.

A Sense of Guilt

Many organ recipients experience feelings of guilt from knowing that they were allowed to live only through another person's death. Some also say they feel guilty for receiving a life-saving organ while others will die waiting. In comments that appear on the Web site WebMD, Dr. Jeffrey D. Punch, chief of transplantation at the University of Michigan, explains: "It's very common for people to feel guilt after a transplant, they think a lot about the donor and feel guilty for bene-fiting from his or her death." Punch adds that feelings of guilt are espe-cially strong in people who prayed and hoped for an organ to come through. Afterward, says Punch, "they feel guilty, as if they were wish-ing for someone to die."

Medawar's description of the immune system was proven correct. This was a victory for science and ongoing efforts to expand knowledge of the human body. In practical terms, however, the operation had little impact. Only a very small percentage of those in need of a kidney have an available identical twin with one kidney to spare. In the case of a diseased heart or liver, having an identical twin would not be relevant at all. Doctors needed to find a way to overcome the immune system so that it would accept an organ from a donor other than an identical twin. Murray and his colleagues speculated that closely matching the cells and tissues of organ donors and recipients might be one way to decrease the severity of rejection.

Tissue-Typing for a Match

During the late 1950s and early 1960s, physicians recognized that compatibility of blood types between donor and recipient was not sufficient to guarantee a successful organ transplant. In an attempt to lessen the number and severity of kidney rejections, researchers began matching as closely as possible the MHAs of both recipient and potential donor.

Researchers headed by Dr. Paul Terasaki at the University of California in Los Angeles learned that each person possesses two basic types of MHAs, called class I and class II molecules. The molecules are complex, consisting of thousands of different combinations, which means that an exact match is highly unlikely. However, tissue-typing within a family, especially between siblings and their parents, can be very close, and doctors recognize that the closer the match, the greater the likelihood for success.

Tissue-typing is performed by drawing a small amount of blood from a potential donor and preparing it for laboratory analysis. Technicians apply specific chemicals to the blood in hopes of revealing the MHAs known to exist in the ill patient. If none or very few are detected, the potential donor is excluded. If a high percentage of matching MHAs is found, even though not 100 percent, the potential donor is considered to be a good prospect. By applying new tissue-matching techniques, surgeons of the 1950s hoped to one day be able to transplant many more organs than just kidneys. Many looked ahead to the possibility of transplanting livers, lungs, and even hearts.

A technician prepares blood samples for tissue-typing to verify the compatibility of a potential organ donor with a recipient.

In spite of improved tissue-typing techniques, the rejection problem continued to surface. In 1963, the National Academy of Sciences reported that only nine patients out of 244 were still alive after organ transplants attempted the previous year. New ideas were desperately needed. Laboratory researchers realized the futility of trying to fool the immune system. They began to think that the best approach might be to simply (and temporarily) suppress it.

Suppressing the Immune System

Initially, doctors tried bombarding the recipient's body with X-rays. The X-rays suppressed the immune system, just as immunologists had hoped, but often the radiation killed the patients as well. Some less devastating procedure was needed. At that time, finding a reasonable solution seemed so unlikely that Dr. Jean-François Borel, a noted Swiss biomedical researcher, rashly lamented, "The concept of organ transplantation seems to be doomed."[15]

In the mid-1960s, however, doctors discovered that a certain class of drugs called immunosuppressants effectively suppressed the immune system without the deadly side effects of X-rays. One of the drugs, Imuran, was initially formulated to fight leukemia, a type of cancer that attacks white blood cells. Imuran contains the compound azathioprine, which decreases the production of lymphocytes. It does this by interfering with the production of the cell's genetic material, thereby preventing the cell from dividing and multiplying. The decrease in the numbers of lymphocytes—especially B and T cells—curtails the immune system's ability to identify and destroy organs containing unfamiliar MHAs.

The use of Imuran to suppress the immune system created one new serious side effect. The suppression of lymphocytes, essential to fight off virus- and bacteria-based diseases, leaves the body susceptible to infectious diseases and death. Patients who received

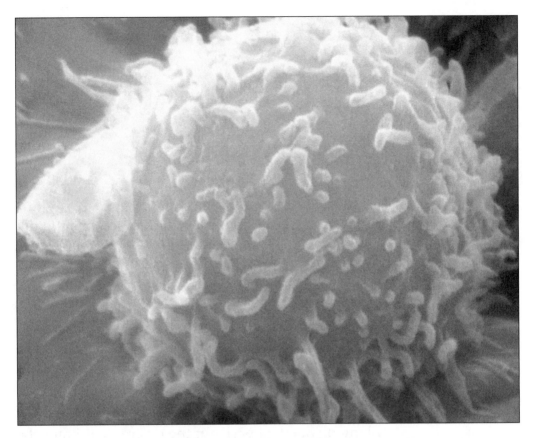

a life-saving organ transplant began dying of common diseases such as pneumonia and the flu, which are normally fought off by their immune systems. Making the use of Imuran even more problematic was the need to use it for the duration of a patient's life.

The availability of the first immunosuppressant, despite its drawbacks, raised hopes among organ transplant surgeons for further success in transplant surgery. It also prepared the way for the next major advance—the first heart transplant, considered the most delicate, complex, risky, and emotionally charged of all the transplant procedures.

Drugs known as immunosuppressants work to decrease production of white blood cells (seen here highly magnified), which are responsible for destroying transplanted organs.

CHAPTER 3

The First Heart Transplant

The handful of successful kidney transplants following the 1954 operation involving the Herrick twins, combined with the discovery of Imuran, heightened enthusiasm among surgeons to transplant more complex organs. But major problems still stood in the way. Most notably, organs such as the liver and heart are far more complex than a kidney. Additionally, each person has only one of each organ, and locating matching donors and performing the surgeries were still daunting.

Highest on the list for the next organ to be transplanted was the heart. Yet the desire to attempt the surgery was tempered by deeply felt reservations. Just fifty years earlier, Dr. Stephen Paget wrote in his book, *The Surgery of the Chest*, "The surgery of the heart has probably reached the limits set by nature to all surgery; no new method and no new discovery can overcome the natural difficulties that attend a wound of the heart." [16]

The heart was the most revered organ. Physicians considered it the most complex organ in the body. Members of the clergy viewed it as the mystical source of each person's spirit. The public saw it as the core of a person's romantic and emotional soul. The idea of cutting the heart out of a person stirred deep emotions, and the thought of replacing it with another was eerie.

44

For these reasons, both medical and cultural, news of the first heart transplant shocked the world. That operation took place on December 3, 1967, in Cape Town, South Africa.

The first heart transplant, like the first successful kidney transplant, represented a culminating event in a

One of the first transplant patients examines his diseased heart preserved in alcohol. The first successful heart transplant took place in December 1967.

series of innovative problem-solving achievements. Before a human heart could be transplanted, logistical concerns had to be addressed. One involved the need to keep the recipient patient alive from the moment the failing heart was removed until implantation of the donor heart. Typically the recipient would be without any heart for about two hours. No one can survive that long without a functioning heart.

The Heart-Lung Machine

A variety of techniques were tested. All included lowering the patient's temperature to between 68° and 79°F

In 1953 John Gibbon used his heart-lung machine on a human patient undergoing open-heart surgery.

(20° and 26°C) below the normal temperature of 98.6°F (37°C). Earlier research had proven that lowering the body temperature slows metabolism, which protects major organs under stress. None of the techniques worked. Eventually, physicians recognized that they would need a machine capable of simulating the action of the lungs and heart. That machine would send oxygen to the blood (as lungs do) and keep blood flowing throughout the body (as the heart does).

In 1950, Dr. John Heysham Gibbon experimented with a prototype of a heart-lung machine (today referred to as a cardiopulmonary bypass machine). His first patients were dogs but in 1953 Gibbon's heart-lung machine was used on a human patient undergoing open-heart surgery.

The cardiopulmonary bypass machine takes over the functions of the heart and the lungs once the diseased heart is removed. The major veins that normally return oxygen-depleted blood to the heart are connected directly to the machine. The machine directs the blood into a reservoir called the oxygenator. There the blood cascades over plastic panels while oxygen bubbles flow through it. As the blood cascades down, its color gradually changes from the dark blue of oxygen-starved blood to the bright red of oxygen-rich blood. The blood is then pumped back into the patient's body at the rate of 4 to 5 quarts (3.8 to 4.8 liters) per minute, roughly the same rate achieved by a normal heart. The cardiopulmonary bypass machine thus does the work of both the heart and lungs, allowing a patient to survive for several hours without a heart.

In the ten years following the first success, Gibbon and others refined the cardiopulmonary bypass machine. Of greatest importance was the introduction of a heat exchanger that cools the blood drawn from the patient, dropping it down to 82°F (28°C) to match the lowered body temperature of the patient. Then, following the completion of surgery, the heat exchanger warms the blood back to normal body temperature. As the blood warms the transplanted heart, it automatically begins beating, although on occasion surgeons must start the heart with an electrical shock. Surgeons check all the connected blood vessels and heart chambers for leaks before removing the patient from the machine.

Gibbon's machine solved one logistical problem. The other involved the organ donor. International laws and ethical standards forbid the removal of a heart from a living donor. The donor first must be declared dead by a physician. This left doctors with the problem of how to keep a donor heart vital once the donor had died. Sometimes the heart needed to be kept alive for days while doctors located a suitable recipient.

The Cadaver Machine

Heart surgeons around the world knew they could not violate the "dead donor rule" that stipulates that no vital organ can be removed from a living person. Yet they also knew that the heart was often uninjured under circumstances in which other vital organs, especially the brain, were destroyed.

Prior to the 1960s, death had been defined as the cessation of a heartbeat and breathing. But at the beginning of the '60s, doctors realized that a healthy heart often stopped only because the brain had died and could no longer signal the lungs to breathe. For this reason, the definition of death gradually changed to focus on whether the brain was alive or not. This change of definition cleared the way for the removal of healthy hearts from people who were identified as brain-dead. Donors typically had suffered brain death resulting from a head trauma in an automobile accident.

To keep a donor heart beating under circumstances like this, researchers developed the cadaver machine (today referred to as a ventilator). This machine is an artificial breathing apparatus that pumps air in and out of the lungs by way of a tube inserted down the throat. As long as the oxygen pumped into the lungs enters the blood, and the heart is uninjured, the heart will pump

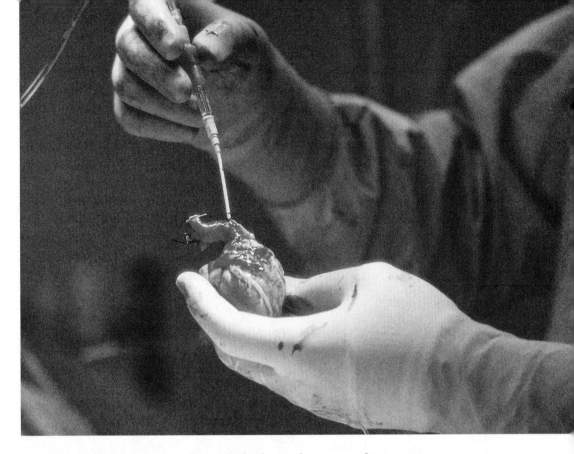

and remain healthy even though the brain has ceased to function. The invention of this machine meant that hearts could be preserved for days until a match was found.

The cardiopulmonary bypass machine and the ventilator solved two major technical obstacles to the first heart transplant. But several years passed before the new technologies could be used in a real-life situation. Doctors first had to locate a heart donor, and finding such a person in the mid-1960s was not as easy as it is today. Many people today designate themselves as organ donors on their driver's licenses. This was not the case forty years ago, so it was much harder to identify a willing donor.

A surgeon prepares a donor heart for transplant. Once cardiologists perfected the transplant procedure in the 1960s, they faced a shortage of willing organ donors.

The Donor Problem

By the mid-1960s, a dozen or so cardiologists were confident that they could successfully perform a human heart transplant. The surgical procedure had been rehearsed on cadavers, the machinery was tested, and immunosuppressants were available to prevent organ rejection. Potential recipients were also plentiful; thousands were dying annually from fatal heart diseases, such as failing heart valves, narrowing arteries, and heart muscle failure. Many volunteered to undergo the first heart transplant, regardless of the risk. The one missing element in the equation was a donor heart.

Doctors had difficulty asking family members for permission to remove the heart of a loved one whose brain had stopped functioning. Family members were reluctant to consent to such a procedure. Parents of a deceased child, for example, were often too distraught about their child's death to consider a request for a heart donation. They had great difficulty responding positively to a doctor asking for permission to remove their child's heart. One doctor who experienced this firsthand was Dr. John Atkinson, at Washington University School of Medicine. He commented, "It's very difficult when a patient is dying to come in and talk with them about using their organs. I find that one of the most difficult things I do as a physician. And it is rarely successful." [17]

Many people then, as well as now, viewed heart donation as a strange and ghoulish act. Some even believed that aspects of the donor's personality might transfer to the recipient along with the implanted organ.

Some of the objections stemmed from religious beliefs. Certain groups of Christians, Jews, Muslims, and members of other religions adhere to ancient strictures that forbid the removal of a person's organs following death. Some people believe that their organs may be necessary for another life at a later time. For others, a dead person's body is considered sacred and particular rituals prohibit the removal of organs. To cut out a heart, even at death, was widely viewed as a sacrilegious act.

As debate continued, several cardiac surgeons were preparing to be the first to perform a heart transplant. Although none had yet located a donor, all knew it was simply a matter of time.

Christiaan Barnard

In Cape Town, South Africa, a young heart surgeon by the name of Christiaan Barnard was pioneering a variety of surgical heart procedures in the 1960s. He had experimented with heart transplantation in dogs and carried out several human heart surgeries repairing valves and suturing holes in the heart chambers. Like other young cardiologists, he hoped to capture the distinction of being the first to transplant a human heart. At that time, about thirty hospitals in America, Europe, and South Africa stood prepared to perform the historic procedure. All had a list of hopeful recipients, but none had a single compatible donor.

In 1967, Barnard had a fifty-five-year-old patient, Louis Washkansky, who suffered from diabetes that was ravaging his heart. Barnard pronounced Washkansky's condition inoperable and predicted that he would not

In 1967 Louis Washkansky, a diabetic from Cape Town, South Africa, received the first transplanted heart.

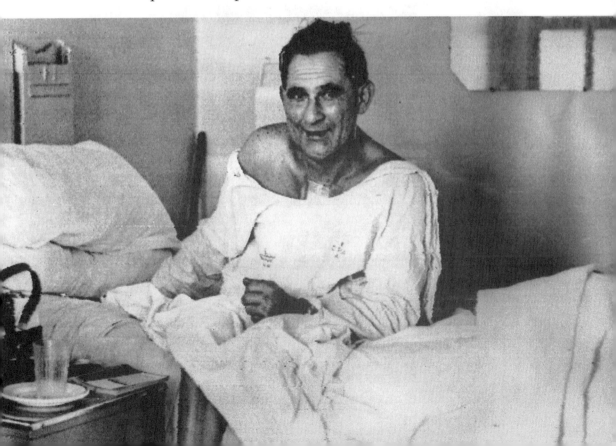

Dr. Christiaan Barnard

Christiaan Barnard was born in 1922 and grew up in South Africa, the son of a poor minister father and housewife mother who played the church organ. Although he expressed little interest in biology or other sciences, his parents insisted that he study medicine at the University of Cape Town. Later, at the University of Minnesota, he developed an interest in the heart while researching cardiopulmonary machines.

In 1962 Barnard returned to Cape Town and accepted a position as a heart surgeon at Groote Schuur Hospital. There he performed surgeries to repair heart valves and tears in heart tissue. He made history in 1967 when he successfully transplanted a heart into his patient, Louis Washkansky.

Barnard never considered the surgery particularly difficult. During an interview with Peter Hawthorne of *Time* magazine, he said, "The heart transplant wasn't such a big thing surgically. The technique was a basic one. The point is that I was prepared to take the risk. My philosophy is that the biggest risk in life is not to take a risk."

South African cardiologist Christiaan Barnard performed the heart transplant operation of Louis Washkansky.

survive to greet the New Year in 1968. Barnard asked if Washkansky would be willing to be the world's first heart transplant recipient in the event that a suitable donor could be located. The surgeon gave the patient an 80 percent chance of surviving the operation but could not say for how long. Recognizing that he had little to lose, Washkansky agreed to the plan. As Barnard later noted, "For a dying man it is not a difficult decision because he knows he is at the end. If a lion chases you to the bank of a river filled with crocodiles, you will leap into the water convinced you have a chance to swim to the other side. But you would never accept such odds if there were no lion."[18]

By early winter in 1967, Barnard was anxious to find a suitable donor. The odds of finding one were slim. A suitable donor would need to have the same blood type and preferably a strong tissue match. He or she would need to have suffered a trauma that caused brain death without injury to the heart, and such a trauma would need to occur somewhere in the immediate vicinity of Cape Town. Most unlikely of all, the family of the brain-dead donor would need to consent to the organ donation, a rare occurrence at that time. Barnard's colleagues estimated that his chances of finding a donor were less than one in a million.

On December 1, as Barnard went about his hospital responsibilities, a twenty-four-year-old South African woman named Denise Darvall was driving home from work. As she turned off a main highway into her neighborhood, her car was struck by a driver who ran a stop sign. Darvall was rushed to Groote Schuur Hospital in Cape Town, the same hospital where Barnard worked. The emergency room physician who examined her declared that bleeding and swelling of her brain precluded surgery to save her life. Because of the nature of the collision, her heart was still healthy. The attending physician placed the unconscious woman on a ventilator and phoned Barnard about her condition. He rushed to examine her.

A blood sample drawn from Darvall turned out to be the same type as Washkansky's. Barnard then ordered tissue-typing to establish whether her MHAs were a close match to his patient's. They were not. Despite the risk to his patient, Barnard moved ahead. He arranged a meeting with the physician attending Darvall and the young woman's parents. Barnard explained that her heart might save the life of another and that such an unprecedented operation would be but the first in a series that would eventually save the lives of thousands of heart patients. Darvall's parents did not hesitate in their decision; they granted Barnard permission to remove their daughter's heart following her death.

Performing the Historic Transplant

The morning of December 3, Dr. Barnard entered the operating room keenly aware of the many uncertainties of performing the world's first human heart transplant. Barnard was anxious whether Darvall's heart would survive while *ex corporeal,* whether all the blood vessels and nerves would attach properly, and whether Darvall's heart would start beating after it was connected to the blood vessels in Washkansky's chest cavity. One of the surgeons assisting Barnard, Dr. Denton Cooley, later confided in an interview:

> One of the most trying times in my career was when we did the first heart transplant. We put it into the patient, and wondered whether it was going to work. Suppose it had not functioned? We weren't certain at all that it would function. [19]

The first of Barnard's critical decisions was to declare Darvall dead. He later recalled, "I did not want to touch this girl until she was conventionally dead—a corpse . . . I felt we could not put a knife into her until she was truly a cadaver." [20] In 1967, most physicians, as well as the public, viewed death as the cessation of the heart and lungs. But when modern inventions such as ventilators were introduced, it was clear that just about anyone's heart and lungs could be kept functioning mechanically even though the brain had ceased to function. In such a brain-dead state, the patient is not conscious or aware of the outside world and incapable of communicating or expressing any sort of intelligent response. Brain-dead patients are commonly referred to as existing in a "persistent vegetative state" that is irreversible.

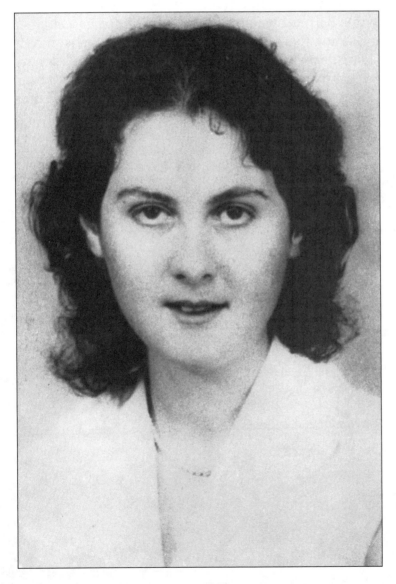

The heart Washkansky received was harvested from Denise Darvall, a twenty-four-year-old woman who lost her life in an automobile accident.

Knowing that Darvall's heart could pump for many days on the ventilator, yet understanding that Washkansky's might not, Barnard declared the woman brain-dead and turned the ventilator switch off. He later recalled that moment: "When we were ready to remove the heart, I turned off the respirator [ventilator] and we waited an agonizing 60 seconds until the heart stopped beating. I remember that clearly."[21]

One surgical team removed Darvall's healthy heart while Barnard walked across the corridor into another operating room and prepared to remove Washkansky's dying heart. After connecting him to a cardiopulmonary bypass machine, Barnard removed his heart, noting later, "I remember when I took the heart out of Louis Washkansky, and inside the chest where there had always been a heart, there was now just an empty cavity."[22]

The surgical team led by Christiaan Barnard operates on Louis Washkansky while nurses ensure the patient remains stable.

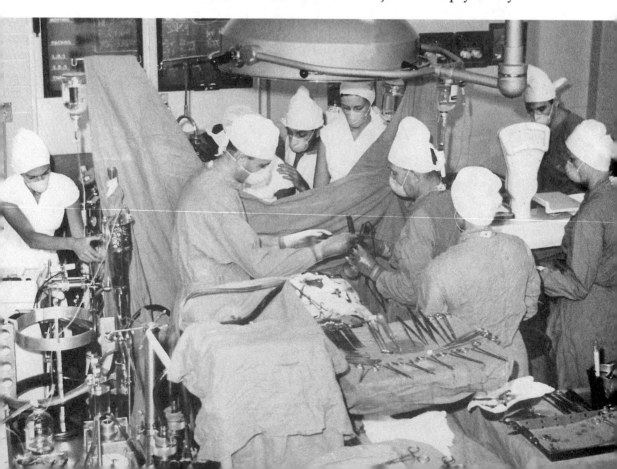

Choreographed Heart Surgery

A heart transplant is a carefully choreographed operation. Everything must be ready so that the surgery can begin the moment the organ arrives. While the donated organ is in transit, the transplant surgical team arrives at the hospital and the recipient is prepared for surgery. The first step is to begin injections of antirejection drugs such as cyclosporine.

As soon as the donor heart reaches the operating room, the surgeon inspects its condition. Any indication that the heart is defective ends the surgical procedure. If it is healthy, the anesthesiologist administers an anesthetic to the recipient and the surgical team takes over.

The chief surgeon begins with the removal of the failing heart. The surgeon cuts an incision down the patient's chest, uses a small circular power saw to cut through the sternum bone, spreads the sternum and ribs to reveal the pericardium (a fluid-filled membrane that surrounds the heart), and cuts it away to reveal the failing heart. With the assistance of surgical nurses, the major heart arteries are clamped, severed, connected to a cardiopulmonary bypass machine, and unclamped. Once the machine takes over, the doctor removes the patient's heart except for the back walls of the atria, the heart's upper chambers. The backs of the atria on the donor heart are opened and the heart is sewn into place. Surgeons then reconnect the blood vessels, allowing blood to flow through the heart and lungs. As the blood warms the heart, it automatically begins beating, although on occasion surgeons must start the heart with an electrical shock.

Darvall's heart was immersed in a cold perfusion of blood and nutrients for twenty minutes and then placed in Washkansky's chest. After completing all sutures and allowing blood to surge into Washkansky's new heart, Barnard hoped the organ would automatically start. But it did not. He waited an extra minute and then applied electrodes to the heart. With the electric shock, it came back to life with a steady one hundred beats per minute. In this five-hour operation, Barnard had successfully completed the first human heart transplant.

Postsurgical Setback

The day after the history-making heart transplant, newspapers around the world carried a photograph of Washkansky enjoying a light meal in his hospital bed. During the next few days, his recovery appeared to be on track, but then his health began to decline.

Knowing Washkansky's immune system would quickly move to reject his new heart, Barnard had begun administering Imuran to his patient the day before the surgery and daily following it. By week's end Washkansky was coughing up mucus and running a fever. The medical team diagnosed the problem as pneumonia and began treating it with massive doses of penicillin. At the end of the second week, Washkansky's condition was listed in the newspapers as "satisfactory" and Barnard told the media that gathered at the hospital, "It's worrying, of course. But I think we can get this infection under control."[23]

But Washkansy's immune system, probably weakened by the Imuran, could not overcome the pneumonia. Eighteen days after undergoing the first human heart transplant, Washkansky died. Despite his patient's death, Barnard viewed the outcome as a success because Washkansky had survived for several days.

> The achievement did not come as a surprise to the medical world. Steady progress towards this goal has been made by immunologists, biochemists, surgeons, and specialists in other branches of medical science all over the world during the past decade to ensure that this, the ultimate in cardiac surgery, would be a success.[24]

Just two months later, Barnard performed a second heart transplant. The patient, Phillip Blaiberg, survived for nineteen months before a heart attack killed him. By the end of 1968, more than one hundred heart transplants had been performed around the world. Like Washkansky, most of the patients died from common treatable diseases because Imuran severely suppressed their immune systems. It was clear at that time that more effective immunosuppressants were needed.

Other problems were also coming to light. New questions about the ethics of heart transplants surfaced. The story of how Barnard acquired Darvall's heart led some to question the whole idea of human heart donors.

The Ethics of Cadaveric Transplants

Following Washkansky's death, medical journals and newspapers were filled with articles expressing outrage at Barnard's treatment of Denise Darvall. Medical ethicists questioned whether Darvall's parents had the

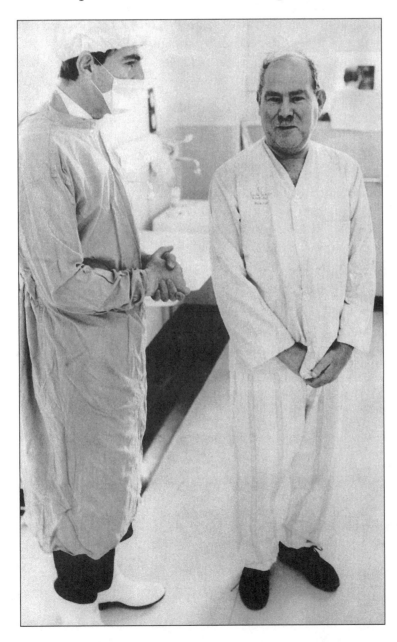

Christiaan Barnard consults with Phillip Blaiberg, his second heart transplant patient, who survived nineteen months with his new heart.

right to donate her heart. They also criticized Barnard's determination of death and his decision to shut off the machine that kept Darvall alive.

Leading-edge medicine frequently creates ethical questions as it moves ahead. Barnard's transplant was no exception. Some of the critics were surgeons who had warned Barnard that he would risk murder charges if he removed Darvall's heart before it stopped beating on its own. Others stated that he had crossed a line by turning off the ventilator. Some religious groups threatened legal action against Darvall's parents for donating her heart. They believed that only Denise Darvall had the right to make that decision.

Of all ethical issues raised, Barnard's decision to turn off the ventilator caused the greatest outcry. Many believed that Barnard turned the ventilator off before Darvall was truly dead. Those critics charged that little clinical evidence had been produced to substantiate the conclusion that she was brain-dead. But Barnard shot back that X-rays of her skull showed severe trau-

Changing Personalities

Some patients contend that they experience distinct personality changes following an organ transplant. The most common manifestation of personality change is called memory transference. With memory transference, an organ recipient seems to acquire some of the personality characteristics, memories, and talents of the donor.

In an effort to learn more about this strange phenomenon, a team of researchers interviewed nearly 150 heart and other organ transplant recipients. Based on these interviews, Dr. Paul Pearsall, a clinical psychologist, proposed the idea that cells of living tissue have the capacity to remember. One recipient, for example, began composing music similar to the music the donor had composed, another started enjoying classical music after receiving the heart of a classical violin student, and an admitted fast food junkie who received the heart of a vegetarian later started vomiting after eating hamburgers. The strangest of all the cases reported by Pearsall was that of a mature woman who received the heart of a fourteen-year-old girl who had been murdered. Following the transplant, the woman was haunted by a nightmare of the girl's murder. She described the man, his clothes, and the weapon to the police, who, based on this information, located and arrested the murderer.

ma, and tests conducted on her by neurosurgeons (including pinpricks to her skin and light shone in her eyes) failed to elicit any reaction. Yet, as Barnard's critics pointed out, there had been patients with severe brain damage who had recovered within days of their injury. Some critics charged that Barnard had killed Darvall in his haste to earn the reputation as the first surgeon to perform a successful heart transplant.

Impassioned ethical debates and the failure to sustain heart transplant patients for more than a few months signaled the need for more research. Researchers in many fields of science went to work to improve rates of survival.

CHAPTER 4

Modern Triumphs

The scientific community learned a great deal from the first heart transplant and many others that followed. One lesson learned was that no one field of medicine could solve all of the problems associated with organ transplants. Scientists representing many fields would need to work together to find solutions. A second lesson, the problem of donor organ shortages, would need to be addressed. Organs would need to be treated with care to guarantee their vitality and used wisely to assist the greatest number of people possible. This latter concern was highlighted and addressed by Dr. Milan Kinkhabwala, professor of surgery at Cornell University, who noted, "Since the biggest problem in the field of transplantation has been organ shortage, advances have been structured around addressing that problem with innovative surgery or alternative solutions."[25]

Perhaps the most pressing problem was the need to suppress the immune system to prevent organ rejection. Because of Imuran and other immunosuppressants, many organ recipients were dying of common illnesses normally detected and eliminated by a healthy immune system. Some better alternative needed to be discovered.

Cyclosporine

During the 1970s, when the surgical procedures for many organ transplants had become relatively routine, many surgeons helplessly watched patients die because Imuran left them vulnerable to illness. The physicians asked pharmacologists to develop more effective immunosuppressants.

In 1972, Jean-François Borel, the same man who ten years earlier had expressed little optimism for transplant patients, was hiking the steep, lush mountain ranges above the fjords in Norway. Expecting to discover nothing more than scenic vistas, he suddenly noticed something very strange just off the path. The fungus *Tolypocladium inflatum* was growing in the dirt, and no other vegetation was growing anywhere around the fungus. The fungus appeared to have killed all plant life close to it. He scooped up a sample and placed it in a plastic bag for later analysis.

A team of surgeons prepares to place a transplanted heart into a patient in 1968. Nearly all early heart transplant patients died within six months of the procedure.

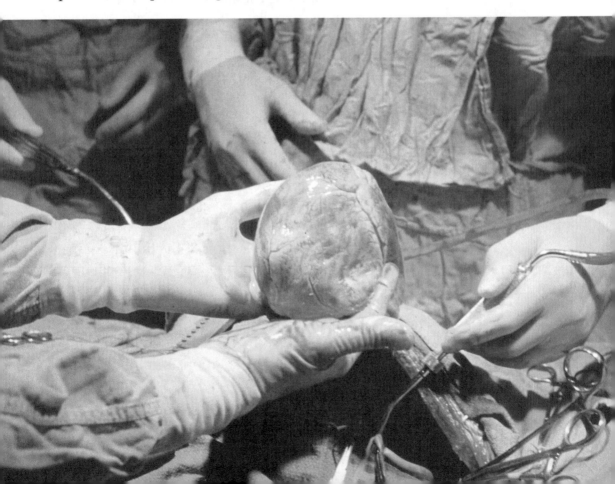

Back in his lab in Switzerland, Borel analyzed the specimen. Soon he discovered why no other plant life grew near it. The fungus produced a by-product called cyclosporine, which had remarkable immunosuppressant properties. It appeared to suppress the growth of all plants around it. What Borel observed made him think that this fungus might be more effective than Imuran or any other immunosuppressant.

Borel tested cyclosporine on rats that had received bone marrow transplants. The results gave the first clinical evidence that cyclosporine might be an important compound. The rate of acceptance of the transplanted bone marrow was quite high, while the suppression of T cells was less than that found using Imuran. This meant that the rats were less susceptible to other common diseases.

Immunologists continued testing cyclosporine on dogs and monkeys undergoing transplants of organs such as kidneys, livers, and hearts. These tests showed remarkable success. By 1976, researchers investigating the effects of cyclosporine concluded that it was a much more effective immunosuppressant than Imuran. Surgeons around the world began using it and reported that their patients were surviving longer and feeling better than ever before.

By the end of the 1970s, cyclosporine had dramatically increased survival rates for heart, kidney, and liver recipients. Acute rejection of the donor organs, which can begin within hours of a transplant, fell from 95 percent to 50 percent. Survival rates after the first year of transplantation rose from 40 percent to 85 percent.

Improved survival rates emboldened more people to undergo organ transplantation, and by the early 1980s surgical rooms were filled with willing patients. Surgeons were also encouraged and began transplanting not only more organs, but combinations of organs, too.

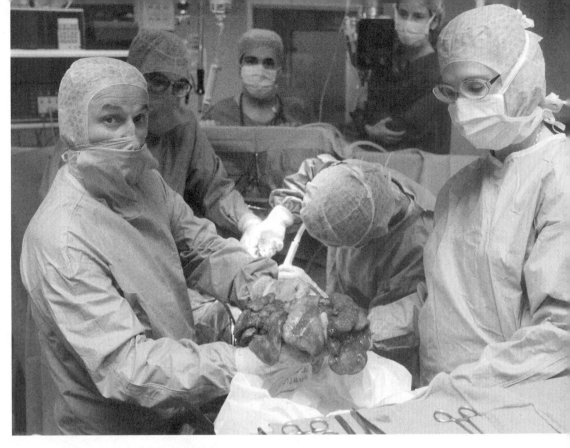

Multiple Organ Transplants

Surgeons had known for some time that the failure of one organ could cause the failure of another. Under such circumstances, patients needed multiple organ transplants. Rather than perform one transplant procedure at a time, each of which involves some risk of death, doctors tried to reduce the risk to patients by performing multiple organ transplants in a single procedure. Heart-lung transplants were the first of these procedures. Heart-liver, double-lung, and heart-liver-kidney transplants followed. The first of these multiple organ transplants took place in the 1980s. By the 1990s, surgeons were taking on transplant procedures of more complexity than ever before.

A triple organ transplant took place at the University of Chicago in 1999. The patient, Kent Slater, was a sixty-four-year-old construction worker who was suffering from a rare ailment called glycogen storage disease. This disease gradually damages first the liver and then other vital organs, such as the heart and kidneys.

Surgeons perform a heart and lung transplant in 1996. The first of these multi-organ transplants took place in the 1980s.

Initially, three teams of surgeons—one for each organ—worked to find suitable donors. Each donor needed to have the same matching blood type and a high degree of tissue matching for MHAs. Those requirements alone eliminated most available donors. But the other requirement, that all three donors (two of which would have to be cadaveric donors) had to be available on the same day in Chicago, appeared to be the most unlikely. After searching for eleven weeks, doctors suddenly located one cadaveric donor, killed in a motorcycle accident, capable of contributing all three organs.

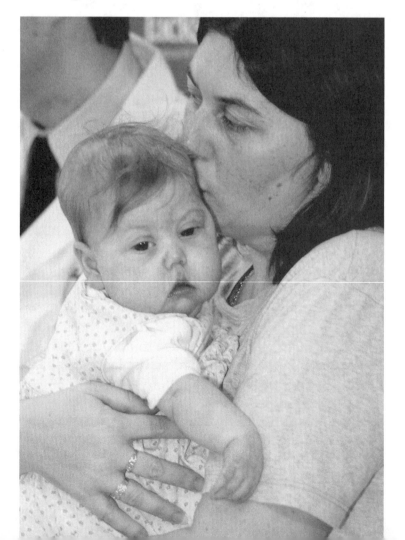

Baby Alessia Di Matteo, suffering from an extremely rare genetic condition, received a record eight organs during a 2004 transplant operation.

The operation took place on May 7. It took fourteen hours and involved a team of eight doctors and eighteen surgical nurses. The triple transplant began about 8:00 A.M. with the heart. The heart had to be the first organ because the brain-dead donor was on a ventilator and the heart was the most vulnerable organ. At 3:30 P.M., the second team of surgeons took over and transplanted the liver, and at 7:30 the third team began the kidney transplant, finishing close to 10 P.M. In the opinion of Dr. Valluvan Jeevanandum, who led the cardiac team:

> A multi-organ transplant like this is a lot like a relay race. To make it work, each team not only has to run a perfect race, but they also need to make a smooth hand-off to the following team. For example, we had to transplant the heart in such a way that it could immediately withstand the stresses of major abdominal surgery, the liver transplant. In this case, each team seems to have "nailed" their leg of the race. [26]

The patient, who is still alive, held the record for the most organs transplanted in a single operation until January 2004, when a seven-month-old baby girl received eight organs. She was suffering from a rare genetic condition called smooth muscle condition. This defect is a potentially fatal disorder that attacks the smooth muscles that line the internal walls of most organs except the heart. It causes the muscles to relax and contract spasmodically, thereby preventing the normal functioning of the affected organs.

Doctors determined that the baby's only chance for survival was to replace her pancreas, liver, stomach, spleen, small and large intestine, and both kidneys. And even then, they gave her only a small chance of surviving. All the donated organs came from a single one-year-old donor. Following the surgery, which lasted thirty-seven hours, doctors reported that their tiny patient was doing well and was eating. Nevertheless, Dr. Andreas Tzakis, the head surgeon, made this cautionary statement to the media: "We are not at ease at all about the baby's condition and we're going to be quite nervous for the first year."[27] Her doctor's concern was well-founded. Several months later, problems developed in the baby's intestines. She died in January 2005 when the transplanted organs failed.

As with all organ transplants, multiple organ transplants had mixed success. Some patients thrived while others did not. Reasons varied for these successes and failures; a sicker patient, for example, would generally be less likely to make a full recovery. Yet in some cases an organ transplant worked even under the most difficult conditions.

The Discovery of the Mystery of Chimerism

For several decades, doctors struggled to explain why some organ recipients showed more dramatic and more immediate acceptance of organs than others. Physicians were eager to explain this mysterious occurrence, known as "high transplant tolerance," in hopes of one day replicating this phenomenon.

In the mid-1990s, researchers found that a small number of kidney and liver recipients did not experience the usual problems with organ rejection. For some reason, donor tissue seemed to coexist with the recipient's own tissue. Scientists named this phenomenon "chimerism," after the chimera, a creature in ancient Greek mythology. This creature had a lion's head, a goat's body, and a serpent's tail. In hopes of unraveling the mystery, scientists performed extensive laboratory analyses on recipients who displayed high transplant tolerance. They discovered that lymphocytes carried over from the donor organs had migrated throughout the recipients' bodies. Even more amazing, the foreign leucocytes coexisted with the recipients' leucocytes without detection by B cells and destruction by T cells; foreign tissue had taken root. Researchers were stunned. For some reason, the normal reaction of an organ recipient's immune sys-

First Organ Transplant Olympian

Snowboarder Chris Klug, a liver transplant recipient, rode his way to a bronze medal in the men's parallel giant slalom during the 2002 Winter Olympics in Park City, Utah. He set a record as the first organ transplant Olympian to win a medal. In 1993, Klug was diagnosed with primary sclerosing cholangitis, the same rare degenerative liver disease that killed Hall of Fame football player Walter Payton in 1999. In 2000 Klug received his lifesaving liver transplant. After five months of therapy, he was back on the slopes.

Klug's donated liver came from a thirteen-year-old boy named Billy Flood, who was accidentally killed by a gunshot wound. The boy's parents made the decision to donate his organs. The boy's mother said she was elated to learn that her son's liver went to an Olympic athlete.

As a demonstration of his appreciation for life, Klug travels the country, encouraging others to donate their organs. In a speech that can be found on Congressman Jay Inslee's United States House of Representatives Web site, Klug said,

> I am here today because of a donor family. Because of this donor family I was able to win great success in the Olympics and all over the world. Being on the organ waiting list was a very scary place to be, but I was very fortunate not to be one of the sixteen people who die every day while waiting for an organ transplant. No one should have to be on the waiting list. My goal is to eliminate the organ donor waiting list—to make that list a thing of the past.

Transplant recipient Chris Klug snowboards his way to a bronze medal in the 2002 Olympics.

tem to detect and destroy the alien tissue appeared to have failed.

Knowing that lymphocytes are produced in bone marrow, surgeons began infusing organ recipients with massive doses of donor bone marrow. They hoped that this treatment would stimulate chimerism in patients who undergo organ transplants. Thus far the procedure seems to be helping. Transplant tolerance is improving, which means that dependence on antirejection drugs following surgery may become less necessary. Doctors view this as an important new development. As Dr. Ron Shapiro explains, "With tolerance [chimerism], we'd be able to taper the drugs or even wean the patient off the drugs completely."[28] While no one knows for certain how chimerism occurs, the results of bone marrow infusion from organ donor to recipient are so promising that

In 1998 Janet McCourt became the first transplant patient to receive infusions of bone marrow from a donor, which has lessened her dependence on antirejection drugs.

physicians now recommend it before all transplant surgeries.

Lack of knowledge and technology posed the greatest challenges in the early years of organ transplants. As knowledge (and experience) grew and technology developed, other challenges arose. One that is still with us today is the shortage of donor organs. As has happened before in the field of organ transplantation, doctors and others have tried to find new ways of addressing seemingly intractable problems like this one. One idea involves organ sharing. Specifically, surgeons are now dividing one liver between two patients in a procedure called a split-liver transplant.

Split-Liver Transplants

One of the unique qualities of the liver is its ability to regenerate damaged tissue. Knowing this, researchers explored the possibility of splitting a healthy liver in half, giving half to one patient and half to another. Once the split livers were transplanted, surgeons anticipated that each half would regenerate and eventually achieve normal size. The objective of this "two-for-one" transplant was to meet the growing demand for livers without needing to increase the number of donors.

Successful split-liver transplants have been done since the mid-1990s. In 1996, several surgical teams in the United States removed livers from cadaveric donors, split them, and transplanted the halves into waiting patients. Surgeons were even able to split an adult liver into two unequal parts, transplanting the larger part into an adult and the smaller into a child. In each case, the transplanted liver segments reached full size within three months.

Split-liver transplants add an additional level of complexity beyond other organ transplants because two recipients are involved rather than just one. This means that both recipients must be in the same hospital, ready for surgery at the same time, and each with his or her own surgical team. The split-liver transplant also raises the risk level because, unlike a full liver transplant, the split livers sometimes leak blood or bile. Of the two, leakage of bile is the more severe problem. Bile is a complex fluid that includes acids used for digestion in the small intestine. If bile leaks onto other organs outside the intestines, it will destroy them.

Hepatologists (doctors who specialize in the liver) have even experimented with splitting a portion of a liver from a living donor. Surgeons reasoned that the same regenerative powers found in split livers from cadaveric donors should be found in a live donor. In 1999, the Mayo Clinic in Rochester, Minnesota, reported the first successful split-liver transplant from a living donor. Doctors reported that the liver segments in both donor and recipient regenerated to normal size and both were fully functional. This was a significant finding because it may eliminate liver shortages altogether. Split livers can regenerate to full size in three to five months. With such a quick recovery rate, doctors speculate that one living donor might one day be able to supply many patients suffering from diseased livers. Dr. Samuel So at Stanford University emphasizes the significance of the split-liver procedure for saving lives:

> The essential message is that this procedure can increase a critically scarce donor pool. The potential number of viable U.S. liver donors is about 5,000 a year, but at any given time, about 7,000 patients are waiting for a liver transplant. About 8 percent of those who are waiting for donors don't live long enough to be transplanted. [29]

Having enough organs to meet the demand is just one part of the supply and demand problem. Another part is getting the organs to the people who need them. Seldom are both donor and recipient being cared for in the same hospital. Donor organs that are transported across country require new technologies to keep them vital for many hours.

Organ Transportation

On many occasions, an organ donor and recipient cannot be brought together for an organ exchange. Even if a man killed in Massachusetts, for example, has an organ perfectly matched to a dying woman in California, the two can rarely be brought together in the same hospital for the transplant. In such cases, the needed organ must be removed and then transported across the country as quickly and carefully as possible. Critical hours go by as the organ makes its way from the donor's operating room to an ambulance, to an airplane, to a second ambulance, and finally to the recipient's hospital.

A young patient gives roses to the woman with whom she shares a transplanted liver. The two were recipients of a successful split-liver transplant.

In 2001 two surgeons demonstrate the Portable Organ Preservation System, a machine that keeps harvested organs viable for hours.

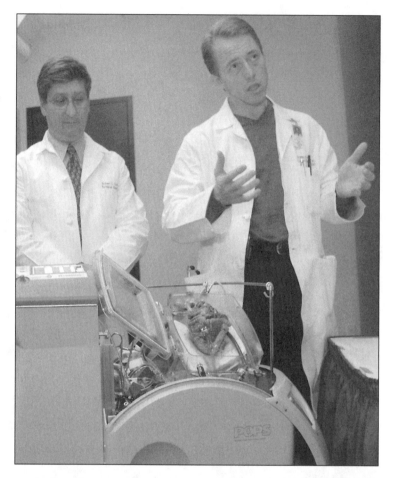

Timing is critical. Some organs must be transplanted more quickly than others, but all must be transplanted within hours of their removal from the donor or tissues will begin to deteriorate. Human organs must be properly stored and enriched during transportation. For organs transported short distances, such as between two hospitals in the same city, a low-tech mode of packaging and transportation is sufficient. The organ is removed from the donor, placed in a perfusion of blood and nutrients, packed in a cooler filled with chipped ice, and rushed by ambulance to the recipient's hospital. The aim is to maintain a temperature just a few degrees above freezing in order to slow tissue decomposition.

Long-distance transportation (from New York to Los Angeles, for example) becomes far more complicated than a cross-town delivery. Until recently, hundreds of organs were lost each year in long-distance transit because either they took too long to transport or because there was no time for the transplant surgeon to evaluate them for viability once they arrived. Surgeons will not risk implanting an organ without first testing the health of its tissues. Today, however, engineers have designed complex systems for organ transportation. These new systems can keep organs fresh for long distances over several hours.

Of several new high-tech organ transportation devices, the Portable Organ Preservation System (POPS) is one of the most sophisticated for long distances. POPS is a computerized traveling environment the size of a large grocery store shopping cart. It has computerized sensors and pumps that can even stimulate a heart to beat while in transit. It is capable of regulating the internal

Placement on the National List

In the early 1980s, Congress and the medical community recognized the need for a nationwide organization to regulate available donor organs. There was a fear that unless organs were regulated, the available organs might be sold on the open market like any other commodity and that only the rich would be able to afford them.

The National Organ Transplant Act, passed by Congress in 1984, prohibited the sale of organs for transplantation. It also created a transplant network called the Organ Procurement and Transplantation Network, which oversees the national list of patients qualified to receive organs and the distribution of available organs throughout the United States. All organs are made available without charge to those on the national list based on a variety of criteria.

Once a qualified recipient is placed on the national list by a physician, his or her vital information is loaded into a database. The patient is notified as soon as a suitable matching donor has been located. Waiting times vary, but the average wait for a kidney in 2004 was 520 days, a pancreas 437 days, a liver 104 days, a heart 245 days, and a combination of a heart and lung, 598 days. Tragically, an average of seventeen patients awaiting an organ die every day because of shortages.

temperature of an organ at precisely 34°F (1°C), infusing the organ with exact volumes of oxygenated blood and other nutrients, electrically stimulating the muscles to contract, filtering the blood, and regulating blood pressure. Because of its revolutionary design, delicate hearts that at one time could survive for only two hours outside the body can now survive for twelve hours. Similar improvements have also been achieved for livers, lungs, and kidneys.

Technological improvements such as POPS have preserved many organs that ten years ago would have expired while in transit. Losing donor organs at a time when too few are available to meet demand has stimulated other solutions to the problem of organ shortages as well. Surgeons have devised ways of rescuing and making use of marginal organs that otherwise might be discarded due to disease or tissue damage.

Rejuvenated Organs

Solving the problem of donor organ shortages triggered the imagination of several doctors but few had more creative ideas than Dr. Abbas Ardehali, director of the Lung Transplant Program at the University of California at Los Angeles (UCLA). In the fall of 2002, a college student in Boston was placed on a ventilator. She was close to death from collapsed lungs. Because of her condition she was not eligible for a donor organ through the government-run organ donor program. The young woman's physician contacted Ardehali and asked if he had any suggestions. Ardehali had established a reputation for being able to repair donated lungs that were damaged and did not meet government standards for transplantation.

Ardehali took the young woman as a patient. He acquired diseased lungs from a donor, cleaned and flushed them with amino acids and nutrients, and implanted them. In May 2003, the young woman finished rehabilitation, returned to college, and confided in an interview, "I'm giddy. It's frustrating I'm not 100

Who Receives an Organ and Who Does Not

The delicate decision determining who receives an organ and who does not is under the control of a computer. Guidelines for screening a match between donor organ and recipient are weighted toward patients with the greatest medical urgency and whose body chemistries most closely match those of donor organs.

To determine which patient will get an organ and from which donor, all sorts of information are loaded into a computer database. This information includes the person's name, location, height and weight, gender, age, status code reflecting the degree of medical urgency (1—the highest level, 2A, 2B, and 3), blood group, blood chemistry, number of previous transplants, and other essential details.

Each time a new donor or recipient is added to the list, the computer program is run to compare donor and recipient characteristics, generating a new list ranking all recipients in order of acceptability. The rankings take into account medical urgency, the best physical match, compatibility of blood types and MHAs, distance between the donor organ and recipient, availability of transplant specialists, and availability of transplant operating rooms.

percent strong because I'm so ready to dive back into life and drink it up."[30] The young woman is presently enrolled in law school.

Since Ardehali's first success at rejuvenating damaged lungs, he and his staff have improved their process and saved many lives that otherwise would have been lost. In a 2005 interview, Ardehali noted that his lung recycling method

> has resulted in an expansion of the donor pool to the point that we are willing to accept lungs that other programs don't feel comfortable with. In fact, of the 27 lung transplants we did last year, about 22 to 24 of them were lungs that were turned down by other programs and would have gone unused.[31]

Dr. Ardehali's approach to recycling rejected lungs was immediately embraced for hearts as well. Dr. Hillel Laks, director of the Alternate Recipient Heart Transplant Program at UCLA, looked into a similar program for reclaiming damaged hearts. Dr. Laks rejuvenates diseased hearts that other hospitals will not accept for transplantation. As an example of the type of repairs Laks makes to hearts, he sometimes performs bypass surgery to improve blood flow on a cadaveric donor heart before removing and transplanting it. As of early 2005, Laks has performed eighty-four transplants using rejuvenated hearts, and his survival rates are comparable to other transplant programs.

Great strides have been made since the first successful transplants and many lives have been extended, yet a surefire remedy for organs beyond repair has not yet been found. In the present state of organ transplantation, it is clear that donor organs are only a temporary fix. Not enough donor organs are available to meet the demand. In 2004, for example, six thousand Americans died while on waiting lists and another one hundred thousand died who did not qualify for any waiting list. Many of those receiving transplants suffer from rejection and the ravaging effects of immunosuppressant drugs. These realities may soon change. Scientists who are presently at work seeking more effective solutions to the problem of organ failure hope to deliver their results within twenty years.

CHAPTER 5

Peering into the Future

Fifty years of research and experimentation since the first successful kidney transplant have taught physicians the fundamental lesson that more effective means for replacing diseased organs must be found. As revolutionary as organ transplants have been over the last five decades, chronic shortages, continuing immune system rejection, ethical challenges, and the extreme side effects of immunosuppressant drugs strongly suggest that better solutions are needed.

Many scientists peering into the future of organ transplants say it is likely that human donor organs will one day be abandoned in favor of more reliable sources of organs. Teams of researchers are already working on new ideas including farms where animals will be bred for their organs and genetically designed for humans use, laboratories for growing needed human organs, more precise immunosuppressant drugs, and mechanical organs. Although most of these projects are a decade or two away from being realized, all are considered reasonable solutions to current problems.

Xenotransplantation

Attempts during the early twentieth century to transplant animal organs into humans failed because too little was known about the surgical procedures and the chemistry of tissues and the immune system. Researchers today, however, say it is time to revisit this medical technology.

Researchers are exploring the possibility of farms for pigs raised exclusively for their organs. Pigs are ideal because they can produce two litters a year, they are easily and inexpensively cared for, and their vital organs are similar in size to those of humans. The pig organs of greatest interest to transplant physicians are the heart, liver, kidneys, and lungs. In the opinion of John Atkinson, chairman of the Department of Medicine at Washington University School of Medicine in St. Louis:

> Pigs are ideal in some ways because their organs are the right size for humans, and the anatomy of the organs is very similar to man. Miniature pigs would be good for children with cystic fibrosis who need a lung, for example, and pigs carry few diseases that can be transmitted to humans. [32]

Medical companies interested in operating pig organ farms are optimistic. One company recently predicted

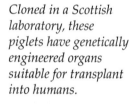

Cloned in a Scottish laboratory, these piglets have genetically engineered organs suitable for transplant into humans.

that by the year 2020, 450,000 pig organs will have been transplanted into humans. Success will depend on solving several problems. Foremost among them is the problem of organ rejection. Xenotransplant researchers are working with geneticists to genetically engineer what they call "perfect pigs." To avoid rejection, these pigs' organs will have to masquerade as human tissue once implanted. To accomplish this feat, researchers will alter some of the pigs' genetic tissues. Speaking about the future of xenotransplantation, Dr. Roger Dobson states:

> It is potentially a useful technology to develop new lines of pigs for xenotransplantation. However, the next step is to see if the technology can be applied to developing genetically modified pigs whose organs can be transplanted into humans without being rejected. [33]

Genetic Engineering

Researchers began working on genetically engineered pig organs for human transplantation in the mid-1990s. New techniques have allowed them to change the genetic structure of an organism's cells. By genetically altering the MHAs of pig organs to more closely resemble human MHAs, scientists believe that rejection can be circumvented and that a new subspecies of pigs will arise exclusively to provide organs for human use.

The genetic alteration would be done before birth, when the pig is still a fetus. Dr. Jeffrey Platt of Duke University explains that the objective is to "overcome the 'foreignness' of animal organs and tissues that leads humans to reject them. If that hurdle can be cleared, there could someday be enough organs to save people who now perish while waiting for transplants." [34]

Several genetic engineering companies in America and Europe are working to raise pigs with MHAs that are compatible with those of humans. Researchers took fertilized eggs out of sows, infused them with human MHAs, and placed them back into the sows. When the genetically engineered piglets were born, they displayed a small amount of human MHA proteins in their genetic structure. Researchers then gave them transfusions of human blood to test for rejection. Results indicate that their organs displayed lower levels of rejection and slower rejection times than the organs of piglets that had not undergone the procedure.

As successes emerge, the idea eventually will be to breed the genetically engineered pigs and then harvest the organs of their offspring. This would create a steady supply of usable organs for people in need of transplants. John Logan, chief scientist for one laboratory experimenting with genetically engineered pigs, says, "The progress around the world in tackling the scientific challenges has been very, very impressive. Several groups are moving very rapidly. I believe it's going to happen."[35]

Scientists engaged in genetic engineering are not alone in the quest for a high-tech solution to the problems of organ transplantation. Another group of molecular scientists has a different potential solution that does not involve pigs. It involves growing new human organs from human cells.

Stem Cell Engineering

Molecular biologists in America and Europe are experimenting with a relatively new technology involving human stem cells. The focus is to use stem cells to create new human organs suitable for transplantation. These unique human cells are the source of each different type of cell in the body. Each person's stem cells are capable of forming all specialized tissue types, including those needed by hearts, lungs, kidneys, livers, blood, and pancreases.

One important source of stem cells is the human embryo. When it is only four days old, the embryo becomes a ball of cells called a blastocyst. The inner cells of the blastocyst are pluripotent stem cells. Pluripotent stem cells can become any cell in the body. These are the cells that hold the most promise for cre-

Baby Fae

In October 1984, a two-week-old baby girl was rushed to the Loma Linda University Medical Center in California. Doctors diagnosed her with a rare defect called hypoplastic heart, a fatal condition in which the left side of the heart is underdeveloped. The baby's identity was kept a secret, but when the media heard about her plight, they told her story to the world and named her Baby Fae.

Baby Fae was placed in the care of pediatric surgeon Dr. Leonard Bailey, who had performed dozens of cross-species transplants on animals. Bailey put the baby in an ice bath to lower her body temperature to 68°F (20°C), thus slowing her metabolism. He then announced that the baby's degenerating condition necessitated the transplant of a five-month-old baboon's heart—the size of a chicken egg—to keep her alive. He extracted the heart from one of the hospital's research baboons. On October 26, 1984, after a four-hour operation, Baby Fae's new heart was functioning on its own.

Along with praise for Dr. Bailey came condemnation. Members of animal-rights organizations, such as People for the Ethical Treatment of Animals, demonstrated at the medical center. Although many religious groups found the sacrifice of animal life for the sake of human life perfectly acceptable, other religious groups disapproved of placing an animal heart inside a human on spiritual grounds.

While ethical debate raged, the baboon heart gave Baby Fae twenty-one days of life before she died on November 15 from kidney failure that led to heart failure. No further primate-to-human transplants were ever conducted.

ating organs that could replace damaged or diseased ones.

One central objective among transplant physicians is to capture some of these pluripotent cells and store them for that person's later use. During storage, the cells must be kept at very low temperatures. Scientists believe that in the future they will be able to thaw a person's stem cells in the event that he or she might need a new organ. Because pluripotent cells can develop into any tissue type, researchers are working to understand how to provide them with the genetic instructions that will trigger them to develop into the needed organ. According to medical correspondent Margo Pietras, writing for Johns Hopkins University, "The theory behind stem cells is that they can be engineered so as to alter their functions. This is done by

A technician stores stem cells in a stem cell bank in London. Using a patient's own stem cells to grow tailor-made organs would eliminate the problem of transplant rejection.

changing the DNA pattern. From this alteration the cells could be used to repair tissue, tendon and bone after injury, heart muscle from heart attack, or cartilage to prevent arthritis. The list of possibilities may change the face of medicine."[36]

Growing a patient's organ from his or her own stem cells eliminates all the current problems with organ transplantation. The organ will have the identical genetic structure and MHAs as its owner, so the problem of rejection will be nonexistent. (This will also make antirejection drugs unnecessary.) British professor Nick Wright of the Imperial Cancer Research Fund states, "We could avoid problems with current transplants where the patient's body rejects the foreign organ."[37]

Stem cell research also has potential for transplanting organs into foreign bodies without the problem of rejection. Because pluripotent cells have not yet begun to develop into a specific tissue type, researchers believe they could be genetically altered to duplicate the MHAs of a recipient. According to science correspondent Christen L. Brownlee, writing for the American Chemical Society, "Tissues created by these methods might be the patient's own genetically, or they could be composed of cells from another donor. They might be swapped for diseased or damaged tissues in the body."[38]

As promising as stem cell research appears to be, an ethical debate swirls about how it is carried out. Recent

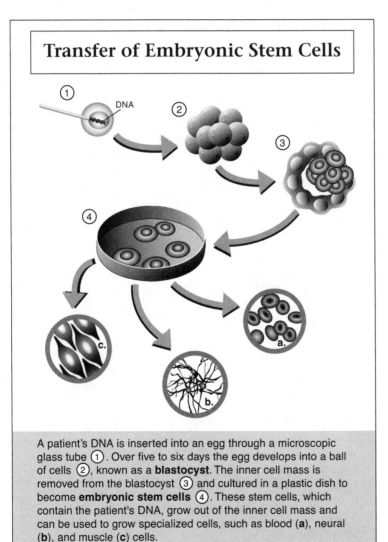

Transfer of Embryonic Stem Cells

A patient's DNA is inserted into an egg through a microscopic glass tube ①. Over five to six days the egg develops into a ball of cells ②, known as a **blastocyst**. The inner cell mass is removed from the blastocyst ③ and cultured in a plastic dish to become **embryonic stem cells** ④. These stem cells, which contain the patient's DNA, grow out of the inner cell mass and can be used to grow specialized cells, such as blood (**a**), neural (**b**), and muscle (**c**) cells.

decisions on the part of President George W. Bush and his administration have restricted research because of the manner in which certain stem cells are gathered.

The Ethics of Stem Cell Research

In August 2001, President Bush decided that the federal government would only fund embryonic stem cell research when that work used existing stem cell lines. No federal money could be used to create new lines of embryonic stem cells. The president opposes the use

The Case of Molly Nash

In 1995, Molly Nash was born with multiple birth defects due to a rare but deadly disease she inherited from her parents (they did not have the disease but carried the genes). Doctors who examined her concurred that her only chance for survival was a perfectly matched stem cell transplant. Her parents did not qualify because each had contributed only half of her genetic composition, nor did cousins or other family members.

In an unprecedented decision in 2000, Molly's parents chose to have a second child. Their primary motivation was to provide a sibling for Molly who could be farmed for his or her stem cells. Molly's mother confided to reporter Rhonda Rowland, writing for the Web site CNN.com, "Jack and I were determined to have more kids, to have more healthy kids, and possibly to have a transplant for Molly."

Creating a second child that would be a perfect genetic match required Molly's parents to create thirty embryos in test tubes. Each was then tested for genetic compatibility with Molly and one was found. It was then implanted into Molly's mother. When she gave birth to this second child, the umbilical cord blood filled with stem cells was set aside. Those saved stem cells were then used to cure Molly of her disease.

Molly Nash (center) sits with her parents and holds the sibling whose stem cells were used to cure her birth defects.

of embryos as a source of stem cells because this process results in the destruction of the embryos. Many of these embryos come from abortion clinics but some also come from in-vitro fertilization clinics.

The president's policy does not affect privately funded research. It only affects research funded by the federal government. Even so, few people are happy with this policy. Opponents of embryonic stem cell research would like to see all of the work with embryos come to a halt. They recommend spending more research dollars on stem cells found in umbilical cord blood and other parts of the body. Supporters, on the other hand, say embryos are the best source for obtaining the type of stem cells that have the most promise. Many of these embryos come from abortion clinics that would otherwise discard them. U.S. senator Orin Hatch made this point in 2001 when he said, "The reality today is that each year thousands of embryos are routinely destroyed. Why shouldn't embryos slated for destruction be used for the benefit of mankind?"[39]

While this debate continues, groups in favor of continuing stem cell research using human embryos are attempting to circumvent the Bush administration ban. In 2004, voters in California approved Proposition 71, a referendum to allocate $3 billion to establish and run the California Institute for Regenerative Medicine. This institute, independent of the federal government, intends to perform stem cell research using human embryos. Private companies are also raising private funds for embryonic research. Opponents of embryonic stem cell research, however, are presently discussing federal legislation to ban all such research within the United States.

Independent of the current stem cell debate, scientists are pursuing other options for growing organs. One that has been of interest to high-tech geneticists recently is the new science of tissue engineering used to grow organs in laboratories.

Neo-organs: Spare Organs on Demand

This new field of science, barely a decade old, involves growing human organs, called neo-organs, in laboratories. Neo-organs are artificial but are grown from a person's own cells. Although this may sound like science fiction, human skin has already been laboratory engineered for burn victims from skin cells taken from their healthy tissues. Because the recipient is also the donor, the MHAs match perfectly and no rejection occurs. The objective of neo-organ technologists is to engineer any needed organ in a laboratory setting and then transplant it.

Tissue engineers who studied how nature forms various structures, such as leaves and coral reefs, recognized that a kind of branching matrix, similar to a scaffold, provides needed support. They then conceived the idea of designing a matrix made of bioabsorbable material (such as that used for sutures), sculpting it to an organ's size and shape, and then implanting it with the desired living organ cells—heart, kidney, lung, or liver. As the cells replicate, they will fill out the three-dimensional matrix, and when seeded in the recipient, the organ will assume its normal functions, whether it is a kidney, liver, or heart.

The organ cells used to build new organs will come from the person in need of the neo-organ—possibly from their stem cells—or from a compatible donor. One of the leading scientists involved in creating neo-organs, chemical engineer Robert Langer, who was interviewed by *BusinessWeek* magazine, said, "Man-made transplantable livers and other complex organs are probably 10 years away, but as the tissue-engineering field gains momentum, miracles may start to come true."[40]

In the event that the many high-tech solutions fail or take too long to produce results, physicians are also trying to improve existing methods. One goal that has been a high priority for many decades is an improved drug that will allow for organ acceptance without rendering the immune system entirely ineffective.

Chemical engineer Robert Langer is one of the leading scientists involved in creating neo-organs.

Selective Immunosuppressants

Immunosuppressants such as cyclosporine shut down the entire immune system, leaving a person's body susceptible to a variety of infectious diseases. Researchers are now working to create drugs that interfere with only those parts of the immune system that detect and attack a donor organ. These drugs, if successful, would assist recipients to accept their new organs without jeopardizing their overall health.

Dr. Polly Matzinger has a new idea about how the immune system works that may lead to improved immunosuppressant drugs. Her research contradicts the older theory that the human immune system differentiates between its own tissue and foreign tissue. In her view, the immune system differentiates between distressed tissue and nondistressed. She believes that damaged cells emit chemical "distress signals" that are then detected by the T cells, activating the immune system. Matzinger thinks that new immunosuppressants can be developed that do not entirely shut down the immune system. She believes that drugs can be designed to selectively suppress the immune system. She points out that T cells are known to receive two types of chemical signals from distressed cells—signal One and signal Two. T cells become activated only

How a Mechanical Heart Works

The IRH, an entirely self-contained mechanical heart, is the result of more than thirty years of engineering research. Its principal advance over the older Jarvik-7 is that patients enjoy total mobility, unlike patients of the past who were tethered to a large air-pumping console by way of wires and tubes piercing their skin.

The IRH is driven by two hydraulic pumps, one for the left and one for the right side of the heart, that move blood from side to side as blood flows to the lungs, back to the heart, and then to the rest of the body. To move the blood, each pump's electric motor spins between 4,000 and 8,000 times per minute. The motor derives power from a small, internal, rechargeable battery implanted on the left side of the abdomen. This battery is capable of powering the motor for twenty minutes. The patient wears a second battery on his or her waist. This battery is used to recharge the internal one, allowing the patient to spend an entire day out of doors.

The moving part of the pump, such as the valves and hydraulic membranes, are manufactured from strong, synthetic materials durable enough to withstand one hundred thousand beats a day, slightly more than a natural heart. The internal walls of the pump are manufactured of polished hard nylon specifically engineered to prevent damage to blood cells and to prevent clotting.

The brain center of the IRH is an implanted, computerized control center the size of a five-volt battery. It automatically adjusts the beat rate and blood pressure of each pump independently by sampling oxygen flow.

when they receive both types. "The solution, of course, is to find drugs that block signal Two without obstructing signal One, and some steps have already been made in this direction."[41]

Implanted Mechanical Organs

While physicians debate the advantages of spending more research dollars on immunosuppressants, tissue engineering, stem cells, or xenotransplants, some engineers believe the best use of research money is not in medicine or genetics, but rather in machines. They believe that the future of organ transplantation may rest with mechanical organs.

Mechanical organs are not new. Dr. Robert K. Jarvik, an American physician, designed his Jarvik-7 artificial heart to function like a natural heart. It had two pumps that pushed the blood from an inlet valve to an outlet valve and throughout a person's body. In 1982, the Jarvik-7 kept a patient named Barney Clark alive for 112 days. The mechanical heart was too large to allow him to leave the hospital and the tubes and wires running through his skin made it impractical, so it was abandoned.

Today, however, interest in a mechanical heart has been renewed. Mechanical and biological engineers have combined their talents to create baseball-sized mechanical hearts that are implanted into the chest cavity and run by small batteries. One of the nation's leading heart transplant surgeons, Dr. Patrick McCarthy, program director at the Cleveland Clinic Heart Transplant Program, predicts, "Mechanical devices will slowly evolve to the stage where they're as successful as heart transplants. Then we will have more options for all of those patients who don't have donors."[42]

In 2001, the first patient received the first completely implanted artificial heart system without any wires or tubes restricting the patient's movement. Surgeons at the University of Louisville in Kentucky implanted the heart in a seven-hour procedure. Named the Implantable Replacement Heart (IRH), the 2-pound (0.9kg) device, made of plastic, titanium, and stainless steel, fills the chest cavity following the removal of a patient's failed heart. Utilizing a battery pack that powers a pump, the IRH moves blood continuously. Patients report hearing the sound of swooshing and humming as the motor spins, rather than the familiar sounds of a natural heart.

Though the first patient did not survive past the first year, a number of the devices have been successfully implanted into other patients. At this time, IRHs have been continuously operating in patients for two years and the objective is to extend that to ten years of uninterrupted use. Representatives for companies manufacturing IRHs believe that their heart systems will eliminate the need for heart donors. As Gerson Rosenberg, chief of artificial organs at the College of Engineering at Pennsylvania State University, states:

> The electric heart will offer advantages over a transplanted heart. There will be no chance for rejection, so people will not need anti-rejection drugs that cause side effects for people with heart transplants. The electric heart could be on the shelf and ready for implantation as soon as the patient needs it. [43]

Physicians at the University of Chicago are in the midst of clinical testing of the first artificial liver device that uses donated cells from humans. The artificial liver, named the Excorporeal Liver Assist Device (ELAD), is a portable blood-filtering device filled with donated human liver cells. It consists of a two-chambered, hollow-fiber cartridge filled with the donated cells through which the patient's blood is passed and cleansed. It is designed to serve as a temporary liver for people until their own liver can heal or until a donor liver becomes available.

Presently the ELAD can be used continuously for up to ten days before it must be removed, refreshed with new human liver tissue, and reinserted. Engineers are

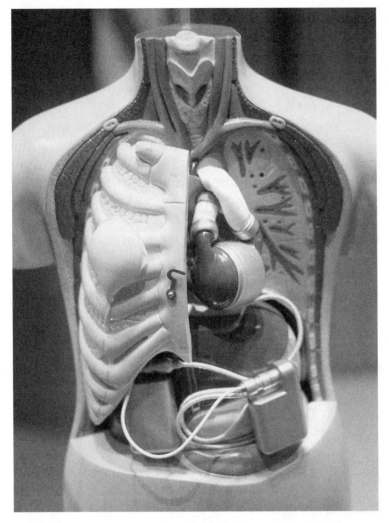

A mannequin shows the Implantable Replacement Heart, an artificial heart used to pump blood continuously through a patient's body.

optimistic about future designs that will be used continuously for more than a month before refreshing the liver cells. Some physicians, including Michael Millis, who is director of the University of Chicago Liver Transplant program, believe that one day the ELAD may entirely eliminate the need for donor livers. He says, "This device has the potential to reduce the need for liver transplants by giving acutely ill patients with limited liver damage time to recover. It could also open the window of opportunity a little wider for those who absolutely need a new organ to survive."[44]

Regardless of the direction that the future of organ transplantation takes, one thing is certain: it will not rely solely on human organ donors. For a variety of reasons, medical, cultural, political, and economic, the science of organ transplantation has never improved to the point where it has been considered a permanent solution to failed organs. Although the technology has improved dramatically over the past fifty years, the major problems of too few donor organs and organ rejection have never been solved. And it is for those two reasons, more than any others, that scientists have moved beyond reliance on human donors in their continuing search for a permanent solution to bodies beyond repair.

NOTES

Introduction: Assisting Bodies Beyond Repair

1. Ronald Munson, *Raising the Dead: Organ Transplants, Ethics, and Society.* Oxford, UK: Oxford University Press, 2002, p. 21.
2. Munson, *Raising the Dead,* p. 264.

Chapter 1: The First Attempts at Transplants

3. Quoted in Julius H. Comroe Jr., "Who Was Alexis *Who?*" *Respiratory Care Journal.* www.rcjournal.com/contents/02.98/02.98.0131.pdf.
4. Quoted in Ole Daniel Enersen, "Alexis Carrel," 2004. www.charleslindbergh.com/heart/index3.asp.
5. Quoted in Nobelprize.org, "Alexis Carrel—Nobel Lecture, December 11, 1912," 2003. http://nobelprize.org/medicine/laureates/1912/carrel-lecture.html.
6. Luis H. Toledo-Pereyra, "Xenotransplantation: A View to the Past and an Unrealized Promise to the Future," *Experimental and Clinical Transplantation,* 2003. www.ectrx.org/ectrx_dergi/dergi_icerik.php%3Ftype%3D2%26index%3D1+Emerich+Ullman+biography&hl=en.
7. Bernard E. Rollin, *The Frankenstein Syndrome: Ethical and Social Issues in the Genetic Engineering of Animals.* Cambridge, UK: Cambridge University Press, 1995, p. 239.
8. Quoted in About Agnosticism/Atheism, "Bioethics: Xenotransplants: Ethics of Transplanting Organs from

Animals to Humans." http://atheism.about.com/library/FAQs/phil/blphil_ethbio_xenotrans.htm.

9. Quoted in Nicholas L. Tilney, "Transplantation and Its Biology: From Fantasy to Routine," *Journal of Applied Physiology*, November 2000, p. 1,689.

Chapter 2: The Problem Within

10. Quoted in Rene J. Duquesnoy, "Early History of Transplantation Immunology," Transplant Pathology Internet Service, http://tpis.upmc.edu/tpis/immuno/wwwHistpart2.html.
11. Joseph E. Murray, *Surgery of the Soul*. New York: Science History, 2004, p. 74.
12. Murray, *Surgery of the Soul,* p. 79.
13. Murray, *Surgery of the Soul,* pp. 77–78.
14. Murray, *Surgery of the Soul,* p. 81.
15. Novartis Transplant, "History of Novartis in Transplantation," 2002. www.novartis-transplant.com/history.jsp.

Chapter 3: The First Heart Transplant

16. Quoted in Margery and Howard Facklam, *Spare Parts of People.* New York: Harcourt Brace Jovanovich, 1987, p. 30.
17. Quoted in William H. Allen, "Farming for Spare Body Parts," *Bioscience,* February 1995, p. 34.
18. Quoted in Public Broadcasting Service, "People and Discoveries: Christiaan Barnard," 1998. www.pbs.org/wgbh/aso/databank/entries/bmbarn.html.
19. Quoted in Academy of Achievement, "Healing the Human Heart," 2005. www.achievement.org/autodoc/page/coo0int-6.
20. Quoted in Hindu Business Line, "The Man Who Gave Heart," 2001. www.thehindubussline.com/businessline/2001/09/07/stories/040734cb.htm.
21. Quoted in British Broadcasting Service, "Health Pioneer Defends Record," 1999. http://news.bbc.co.uk/1/hi/health/523505.stm.

22. Quoted in British Broadcasting Service, "Health Pioneer Defends Record."

23. Quoted in *Time*, "Progress, Then Setback," December 22, 1967. www.time.com/time/archive/preview/ 0,10987,899915,00.html.

24. Quoted in Sat Sharma and Helmut Unruh, "History of Adult Transplantation," *Emedicine*, 2004. www. emedicine.com/med/topic3497.htm.

Chapter 4: Modern Triumphs

25. Quoted in Barbara A. Gabriel, "Organ Transplantation: Modern Triumphs—and Tribulations," Association of American Medical Colleges, 2005. www.aamc.org/ newsroom/reporter/june03/transplants.htm.

26. Quoted in University of Chicago Hospitals, "University of Chicago Surgeons Perform Heart-Liver-Kidney Transplant," 1999. www.uchospitals.edu/news/1999/ 19990511-tx3.php.

27. Quoted in Marylin Peters, "Baby Has Eight-Organ Transplant," Marylin's Transplant Page, March 2004. www.marylinstransplantpage.org/baby-has04.htm.

28. Quoted in Organ Transplant Association, "Chimerism," February 2002. http://organtx.org/chim.htm.

29. Quoted in Hepatitis-C, "Some Information about Split Liver Transplants," 1996. http://hepatitis-c.de/split.htm.

30. Quoted in Ask Emilyss, "Doctor's Eye Damaged Organs for Some Transplant Patients," May 2003. http:// www.askemilyss.com/bites/bite0503/organs.htm.

31. Quoted in Gabriel, "Organ Transplantation: Modern Triumphs—and Tribulations."

Chapter 5: Peering into the Future

32. Quoted in Allen, "Farming for Spare Body Parts," p. 107.

33. Roger Dobson, "Cloning of Pigs Brings Xenotrans-plants Closer," *British Medical Journal*, March 25, 2000, p. 826.

34. Quoted in *CNN*, "Not a Pig in a Poke: Genetic Engineering Could Overcome Rejection Problems,"

April 1997. www.cnn.com/HEALTH/9704/28/nfm.
pig.transplants.

35. Quoted in Allen, "Farming for Spare Body Parts,"
p. 108.

36. Margo Pietras, "New Cellular Engineering Department
at Hopkins," Johns Hopkins University, March 2001.
www.jhu.edu/~newslett/03-1-01/Science/1.html.

37. Quoted in David Whitehouse, "Stem Cells Promise
Liver Repair," BBC News, July 2000. http://news.bbc.
co.uk/1/hi/sci/tech/841932.stm.

38. Christen L. Brownlee, "The Mechanics of Tissue
Engineering," *American Chemical Society Publications,*
2001. http://pubs.acs.org/subscribe/journals/mdd/
v04/i12/html/12brownlee.html#auth.

39. Quoted in CNN News, "Research Foes Decry Embryo
'Slaughter,'" July 2001. http://archives.cnn.com/
2001/HEALTH/07/17/stem.cell.hearing/.

40. Quoted in Catherine Arnst, "The Dynamic-Duo of
Tissue Engineering," *BusinessWeek Online,* 1998.
www.businessweek.com/1998/30/b3588008.htm.

41. Polly Matzinger, "The Real Function of the Immune
System," Center for Molecular Medicine and Genetics,
Wayne State University School of Medicine. http://
cmmg.biosci.wayne.edu/asg/polly.html.

42. Quoted in Gabriel, "Organ Transplantation: Modern
Triumphs—and Tribulations."

43. Quoted in "Artificial Heart," American Society of
Mechanical Engineers. www.asme.org/eyewitness/
heart/heartintro.html.

44. Quoted in University of Chicago Hospitals, "Trial
Begins for First Artificial Liver Device Using Human
Cells," 1999. www.uchospitals.edu/news/1999/1999
0225-elad.php.

FOR FURTHER READING

Books

Christiaan Barnard, *Christiaan Barnard: One Life.* Edinburgh, Scotland: Harrap, 1969. This autobiography was written shortly after the author performed the first heart transplant. It chronicles his youth, his interest in surgery, the Washkansky transplant, and his personal life following the fame that resulted from the operation.

Margery and Howard Facklam, *Spare Parts for People.* New York: Harcourt Brace Jovanovich, 1987. This is an excellent book for young audiences that discusses all major transplants topics. It provides an excellent overview of this medical field.

Reg Green, *The Nicholas Effect: A Boy's Gift to the World.* Sebastopol, CA: O'Reilly, 1999. This book is a poignant account of a California boy's murder in 1994 while vacationing with his family in Italy. It tells the story of his parents' grief and their willingness to donate seven of their son's organs to seven strangers all living in Italy.

Chris Klug, *To the Edge and Back: My Story from Organ Transplant Survivor to Olympic Snowboarder.* New York: Carroll & Graf, 2004. Klug tells the story of his near-death from liver failure and the transplant that saved his life and made it possible for him to eventually win a medal in the Winter Olympics.

Joseph E. Murray, *Surgery of the Soul.* New York: Science History, 2004. This book is an autobiography detailing the highlights of Murray's life. Chapter nine discusses his landmark kidney transplant.

Elizabeth Parr and Janet Maze, *Coping With an Organ Transplant: A Practical Guide to Understanding, Preparing For, and Living With an Organ Transplant*. New York: Penguin Putnam, 2001. The authors provide a simple introduction to organ transplants. They discuss a variety of topics including how transplant candidates are chosen, preparations for transplant surgery, dealing with organ rejection, and what is involved in long-term recovery.

Nicholas L. Tilney, *Transplant: From Myth to Reality*. New Haven, CT: Yale University Press, 2003. Tilney is a surgeon who provides fascinating insights into organ surgery. His style is engaging and the text filled with amusing stories along with photographs taken in the operating room.

Web Sites

Children's Organ Transplant Association (www.cota.org). This Web site is both a fund-raising site for children in need of organ transplants and a source of information about the unique needs of children donors and recipients.

How Organ Transplants Work (http://health.howstuff works.com/organ-transplant.htm). This site is intended for young audiences. It discusses the different organs that are transplanted, the surgery, waiting lists, and what life is like while waiting for an organ.

Organ Transplant Association (http://organtx.org). This site is a comprehensive resource for all aspects of organ transplantation. It provides links to dozens of topics relating to organ transplants.

Works Consulted

Books

Arthur L. Caplin and Daniel H. Coelho, *The Ethics of Organ Transplants: The Current Debate*. Amherst, NY: Prometheus, 1998. The authors selected thirty-five articles highlighting current ethical debates related to organ transplantation.

Renée C. Fox and Judith P. Swazey, *Spare Parts: Organ Replacement in American Society*. Oxford, UK: Oxford University Press, 1992. The focus of this book is the development of organ transplantation during the 1980s and early 1990s. The authors provide detailed information on the many failures as well as the successes, the ethical controversies, and the first attempts at using the mechanical heart named the Jarvik-7.

David Lamb, *Organ Transplants and Ethics*. London: Routledge, 1990. Lamb provides a detailed study of several current ethical problems linked with donor implants. He covers many topics but focuses primarily on the use of cadaveric and living organ donors.

Ronald Munson, *Raising the Dead: Organ Transplants, Ethics, and Society*. Oxford, UK: Oxford University Press, 2002. Munson provides an introduction to a variety of ethical issues surrounding organ transplantation. With a minimum of technical terminology, he discusses the definition of death, methods for obtaining organs, recipient selection, xenotransplantation, and stem cell research.

Bernard E. Rollin, *The Frankenstein Syndrome: Ethical and Social Issues in the Genetic Engineering of Animals.* Cambridge, UK: Cambridge University Press, 1995. This book covers the history of the use of animals for medical experimentation. The author discusses medical and moral issues and problems arising from using animals for research and organ transplantation.

Periodicals

William H. Allen, "Farming for Spare Body Parts," *Bioscience,* February 1995.

Roger Dobson, "Cloning of Pigs Brings Xenotransplants Closer," *British Medical Journal,* March 25, 2000.

David J. Mooney and Antonios G. Mikos, "Growing New Organs," *Scientific American,* April 1999.

Nicholas L. Tilney, "Transplantation and Its Biology: From Fantasy to Routine," *Journal of the Applied Physiology,* November 2000.

Internet Sources

About Agnosticism/Atheism, "Xenotransplants: Ethics of Transplanting Organs from Animals to Humans." http://atheism.about.com/library/FAQs/phil/blphil_ethbio_xenotrans.htm.

Academy of Achievement, "Dr. Willem J. Kolff: Pioneer of Artificial Organs," 2004. http://209.146.26.198/teachers/icdv2i2s/SITES/ACHIEVE/ko10pro_.htm.

———, "Healing the Human Heart," 2005. www.achievement.org/autodoc/page/coo0int-6.

J. Akerman, "The Nobel Prize in Physiology or Medicine 1912," Nobelprize.org, 1912. http://nobelprize.org/medicine/laureates/1912/press.html.

American Society of Mechanical Engineers, "Artificial Heart." www.asme.org/eyewitness/heart/heartintro.html.

American Society of Nephrology, "ASN Celebrates 50th Anniversary of First Kidney Transplant: Experts Reflect on Major Advances and Look Ahead to the Future of

Transplants," The American Society of Nephrology, 2004. www.asn-online.org/media/pdf/2004-Media/ 50th%20AnniversaryTransplant%20Release.pdf.

Catherine Arnst, "The Dynamic-Duo of Tissue Engineering," *BusinessWeek Online*, 1998. www.businessweek.com/ 1998/30/b3588008.htm.

Ask Emilyss, "Doctor's Eye Damaged Organs for Some Transplant Patients," May 2003. www.askemilyss. com/bites/bite0503/organs.htm.

British Broadcasting Service, "Health Pioneer Defends Record," 1999. http://news.bbc.co.uk/1/hi/health/ 523505.stm.

Christen L. Brownlee, "The Mechanics of Tissue Engineering," *American Chemical Society Publication,* 2001. http://pubs.acs.org/subscribe/journals/mdd/ v04/i12/html/12brownlee.html#auth.

CNN News, "Not a Pig in a Poke: Genetic Engineering Could Overcome Rejection Problems," April 1997. www.cnn. com/HEALTH/9704/28/nfm.pig.transplants.

———, "Research Foes Decry Embryo 'Slaughter,'" July 2001. http://archives.cnn.com/2001/HEALTH/07/17/ stem.cell.hearing/.

Julius H. Comroe Jr., "Who Was Alexis *Who?" Respiratory Care Journal.* www.rcjournal.com/contents/02.98/01 31.pdf.

Rene J. Duquesnoy, "Early History of Transplantation Immunology," Transplant Pathology Internet Service. http://tpis.upmc.edu/tpis/immuno/wwwHistpart2. html.

Ole Daniel Enersen, "Alexis Carrel," 2004, *Charles Lindberg.* www.charleslindbergh.com/heart/index3.asp.

Barbara A. Gabriel, "Organ Transplantation: Modern Triumphs—and Tribulations," Association of American Medical Colleges, 2005. www.aamc.org/newsroom/ reporter/june03/transplants.htm.

Peter Hawthorne, "Heart to Heart," *Time.* www.time. com/time/archive/preview/0,10987,1000697,00.html.

Hepatitis-C, "Some Information about Split Liver Transplants," 1996. http://hepatitis-c.de/split.htm.

Hindu Business Line, "The Man Who Gave Heart," 2001. www.thehindubusinessline.com/businessline/2001/09/07/stories/040734cb.htm.

Jay Inslee, "Olympic Medalist Chris Klug Joins Inslee to Introduce Organ Donor Legislation," United States House of Representatives, April 2002. www.house.gov/inslee/issues/health/organ_donor_klug.html.

Polly Matzinger, "The Real Function of the Immune System," Center for Molecular Medicine and Genetics, Wayne State University School of Medicine. http://cmmg.biosci.wayne.edu/asg/polly.html.

Nobelprize.org, "Alexis Carrel—Nobel Lecture, December 11, 1912," 2003. http://nobelprize.org/medicine/laureates/1912/carrel-lecture.html.

Novartis Transplant, "History of Novartis in Transplantation," 2002. www.novartis-transplant.com/history.jsp.

Organ Transplant Association, "Chimerism," February 2002. http://organtx.org/chim.htm.

Marylin Peters, "Baby Has Eight-Organ Transplant," Marylin's Transplant Page, March 2004. www.marylinstransplantpage.org/baby-has04.htm.

Margo Pietras, "New Cellular Engineering Department at Hopkins," Johns Hopkins University, March 2001. www.jhu.edu/~newslett/03-1-01/Science/1.html.

Public Broadcasting Service, "People and Discoveries: Christiaan Barnard," 1998. www.pbs.org/wgbh/aso/databank/entries/bmbarn.html.

Rhonda Rowland, "Genetic Testing of Embryos Raises Ethical Issues," CNN.com, June 2001. http://archives.cnn.com/2001/HEALTH/06/27/embryo.testing.

Sat Sharma and Helmut Unruh, "History of Adult Transplantation," *Emedicine*, 2004. www.emedicine.com/med/topic3497.htm.

Time, "Progress, Then Setback," December 22, 1967. www. time.com/time/archive/preview/0,10987,899915, 00.html.

Luis H. Toledo-Pereyra, "Xenotransplantation: A View to the Past and an Unrealized Promise to the Future," *Experimental and Clinical Transplantation*, 2003. www. ectrx.org/ectrx_dergi/dergi_icerik.php%3Ftype%3D2% 26index%3D1+Emerich+Ullman+biography&hl=en.

University of Chicago Hospitals, "Trial Begins for First Artificial Liver Device Using Human Cells," 1999. www.uchospitals.edu/news/1999/19990225-elad.php.

———, "University of Chicago Surgeons Perform Heart-Liver-Kidney Transplant," 1999. www.uchospitals. edu/news/1999/19990511-tx3.php.

Susan Watts, "Cell Success Has Huge Potential," BBC News, November 1998. http:/news.bbc.co.uk/1/hi/ sci/tech/208497.stm.

WebMD, "Life After Your Transplant: Coping Emotionally." http://aolsvc.health.webmd.aol.com/content/article/ 97/104124.htm?z=1667_104599-2752_HZ_08.

David Whitehouse, "Stem Cells Promise Liver Repair," BBC News, July 2000. http://news.bbc.co.uk/1/hi/ sci/tech/841932.stm.

INDEX

Picture Credits

About the Author

James Barter resides in Rancho Santa Fe, California, and lectures throughout the San Diego area.